Contents

Acknowledgments

This book has been compiled with the co-operation of several organisations, including other government departments and agencies. The editor would like to thank all those who have contributed their comments, and in particular The Scottish Office, Scottish Enterprise, Highlands and Islands Enterprise, and the Scottish Sports Council.

Photograph Credits

Numbers refer to the pages of the illustration section (1–8): Still Moving Picture Company p. 1 (top), p. 2 (bottom), p. 7 (bottom), p. 8 (all pictures); COI Picture Library p. 1 (bottom), p. 6 (top and bottom; BP p. 2 (top); The Scotch Whisky Association p. 3 (top); The Strathclyde Passenger Transport Executive p. 3 (bottom); The Forestry Commission p. 7 (top).

Scotland

London: H M S O

Researched and written by Reference Services, Central Office of Information.

This publication is an expanded and updated version of a booklet with the same title previously published by the Foreign & Commonwealth Office.

ISBN 0 11 701728 0

HMSO publications are available from:

HMSO Publications Centre
(Mail, fax and telephone orders only)
PO Box 276, London SW8 5DT
Telephone orders 071-873 9090
General enquiries 071-873 0011
(queuing system in operation for both numbers)
Fax orders 071-873 8200

HMSO Bookshops
49 High Holborn, London WC1V 6HB   071-873 0011
Fax 071-873 8200 (counter service only)
258 Broad Street, Birmingham B1 2HE   021-643 3740   Fax 021-643 6510
Southey House, 33 Wine Street, Bristol BS1 2BQ
0272 264306   Fax 0272 294515
9-21 Princess Street, Manchester M60 8AS   061-834 7201   Fax 061-833 0634
16 Arthur Street, Belfast BT1 4GD   0232 238451   Fax 0232 235401
71 Lothian Road, Edinburgh EH3 9AZ   031-228 4181   Fax 031-229 2734

HMSO's Accredited Agents
(see Yellow Pages)

and through good booksellers

Introduction

Scotland has a population of around 5 million and comprises approximately one-third of the land area of the United Kingdom.[1] For nearly three centuries Scotland has been united politically with England and Wales and their economies have long been integrated. However, Scotland has retained a strong sense of national identity as well as many distinctive characteristics and institutions.

Ministerial responsibility for most matters affecting Scotland rests with the Secretary of State for Scotland—a member of the Cabinet of the British Government—whose duties are discharged principally through the five departments of The Scottish Office. These are based in Edinburgh and deal with a wide range of domestic, social and economic affairs.

In the House of Commons specially constituted committees consider matters of particular concern to Scotland, and separate Acts of Parliament are passed for Scotland on many domestic issues. Special provisions applying to Scotland alone are also inserted in Acts which otherwise apply to Britain generally. Proposals for legislative devolution, involving the establishment of a Scottish Assembly with responsibility for a wide range of domestic affairs, were embodied in the Scotland Act 1978. Under the terms of the Act a referendum was held in March 1979, but the required majority was not achieved and the Act was repealed.

Significant changes in the Scottish economy have occurred in recent decades, with development of the new technology industries

[1]The United Kingdom—or Britain, as it is known informally—consists of England, Wales, Scotland and Northern Ireland. Great Britain comprises England, Wales and Scotland.

and considerable growth in the service sector. A major influence has been the discovery and exploitation of oil and gas resources in the continental shelf under the North Sea, with much of the oil and gas being brought ashore in Scotland. Investment from overseas is also playing an important part, particularly in manufacturing.

Tourism has become an increasingly important industry, with a large number of visitors attracted by the beauty and variety of Scotland's countryside and coast, the many sites of historical interest, and the opportunities for a range of sports and recreations. The need to protect the land from uncontrolled industrial and other development is widely recognised, and many organisations are working, with government co-operation, to preserve and improve the environment in urban centres and in the countryside.

The education system aims to provide children with a broad and balanced curriculum which offers opportunities for specialisation as well as technical and vocational training in preparation for future employment.

Scotland has a distinguished cultural and artistic heritage. Two of Britain's foremost cultural events are the annual Edinburgh International Festival of Music and Drama, and the Glasgow Mayfest. For 1990 Glasgow was designated as the European City of Culture.

The royal family has close ties with Scotland. On State occasions the Queen uses Holyroodhouse in Edinburgh and privately she spends a proportion of each year at the royal residence of Balmoral in Grampian. The Prince of Wales and some other members of the royal family were educated at Gordonstoun in north-east Scotland.

This book gives an outline of the political, economic and social structure in Scotland including the Government's policies as they affect Scotland. More detailed information on particular subjects, including government policy, is given in the relevant title in the *Aspects of Britain* series. [A list of titles in print is given on the inside back cover.] Further information is also available in *Current Affairs—A Monthly Survey*, published by HMSO.

The Country and the People

Scotland is bounded in the north and west by the Atlantic Ocean, and in the east by the North Sea. The mainland stretches 440 km (275 miles) from north to south, has a maximum width of 248 km (154 miles) and is fringed by numerous islands, of which the principal groups are the Orkney and Shetland Islands to the north and the Hebrides to the west. The total area is 78,800 sq km (30,420 sq miles), representing 32 per cent of the area of Britain. The area comprises some 77,100 sq km (30,000 sq miles) of land and 1,700 sq km (660 sq miles) of inland water. The coastline, including that of the islands, measures some 10,100 km (6,300 miles).

The landscape has many contrasts: mountains and lowlands; deep glens (narrow valleys) and coastal plains; as well as forests, rivers and lochs (lakes). On the Atlantic side long inlets penetrate the land, forming sea lochs, while on the east coast the North Sea has eroded the softer sands and formed wide estuaries. The country is divided broadly into three regions:

—The Highlands and Islands in the north and west account for just over half of the total area and contain the most ancient of Britain's geological formations and some of the highest mountains. Ben Nevis, at 1,343 m (4,406 ft), is the highest in Britain.

—The Central Lowlands, comprising a tract of undulating country with several hill ranges, contains the main centres of population and industry as well as fertile farmlands.

—The Southern Uplands, including the Border Country, is a largely agricultural and pastoral area.

Scotland's climate is temperate, influenced by the Gulf Stream from the North Atlantic. Rainfall varies from an annual average of about 190 cm (80 inches) in the mountainous parts of the north and west to 75 cm (30 inches) in the east. During some winters the upland areas, particularly the Highlands, experience heavy snowstorms with severe drifting. A feature of the summer is the long twilight. In the far north there is no complete darkness at midsummer.

History

The Roman occupation of Britain in the first century AD did not extend north of Hadrian's Wall, which the Romans built between the rivers Solway and Tyne in England. By the beginning of the sixth century Scotland is known to have been divided among four peoples:

—Picts, mainly from north of the Forth-Clyde line;

—Scots, who had crossed from Ireland to settle in Argyll;

—Welsh Britons, driven north by invaders of England to settle in the Strathclyde area; and

—Angles, who settled in Lothian, south of the Forth estuary, at that time part of the Kingdom of Northumbria.

The Scots and the Britons, both of Celtic origin, were Christian. Christianity came to the Picts, and subsequently to the Angles, following the arrival in Scotland of the Irish monk Columba, who landed on the island of Iona in the Inner Hebrides in 563.

Clashes between these peoples were rife until 844, when in response to attacks from the Vikings, a united kingdom of Picts and Scots, known as Albyn or Alba, was proclaimed under the Scots' king Kenneth MacAlpin. The union was later extended to include the Britons of Strathclyde and in 1025 Lothian was formally ceded to Scotland by Northumbria. Malcolm II, King of Albyn, became the first monarch of an area approximating to modern mainland Scotland.

The establishment of a powerful monarchy in England, following the Norman Conquest in the eleventh century, posed an intermittent but considerable threat to Scottish independence throughout the Middle Ages. Towards the end of the thirteenth century Edward I of England attempted to bring Scotland under his rule. In the ensuing struggle for independence Robert Bruce, crowned King of Scots in 1306, led an army to victory over English forces at Bannockburn in 1314. This paved the way for the Treaty of Northampton in 1328, which formally established Scotland's national independence.

The accession to the Scottish throne in 1542 of the infant Mary Stuart, brought up in France as a Roman Catholic, coincided with the establishment in Scotland of the Reformed Church, led by the Calvinist (Protestant) John Knox. Religious and civil strife occurred in Mary's reign, which ended with the defeat of her supporters in 1568 and her flight to England, where she was imprisoned by Queen Elizabeth I and executed 19 years later on charges of conspiracy.

Following the death in 1603 of Elizabeth, who had no heirs, the Protestant James Stuart, Mary's son, whose grandmother was a sister of Henry VIII, succeeded to the throne of England. Although the monarchies were united in the person of the King (James VI of Scotland, James I of England), the Scottish and English kingdoms remained separate entities during the seventeenth century (except for an enforced unification from 1649 to 1660 by Oliver Cromwell following his defeat of royalist forces in Scotland). By the beginning of the eighteenth century, however, political and economic arguments for a closer union were making themselves heard in both countries. Eventually, in 1707, after lengthy negotiations, the two sides agreed on the formation of a single parliament for Great Britain. Scotland retained its own legal, educational and ecclesiastical systems.

In 1714 Queen Anne died without a direct heir, and George, Elector of Hanover (descended from a daughter of James VI/I), succeeded to the British throne. 'Jacobite' uprisings took place in 1715 and 1745 on behalf of the Catholic Stuart claimants to the throne (descendants of James VII/II, who was overthrown in 1688), attracting much of their support from the Highlands of Scotland. The Jacobite cause was finally lost at the battle of Culloden in 1746, the last land battle to be fought in Britain.

An era of stability and economic progress followed, with many scientific and artistic achievements. Agricultural land was reclaimed and drained, farms properly laid out, and livestock breeds developed and improved. The whisky industry began to expand, and spectacular advances were made in coalmining, textile production, iron and steel manufacture, heavy engineering and shipbuilding.

The concept of universal education had been accepted in Scotland as early as the sixteenth century, long before such views were prevalent in any other part of Britain. At the end of the seventeenth century the Scottish Parliament enacted that every parish should provide a school and the salary for a teacher. A solid foundation of educational provision therefore existed in Scotland by the time of the great expansion of education towards the end of the nineteenth century.

Scotland has produced many men and women of distinction and achievement. Among names distinguished in the arts and humanities are those of the poet Robert Burns (1759–96); the novelist Sir Walter Scott (1771–1832), who had a profound influence on European literature, and the author Robert Louis Stevenson (1850–94). Major figures in the field of architecture were the Adam brothers, Robert (1723–92) and James (1730–94), exponents of the neo-classical style, and the innovative Charles Rennie Mackintosh (1868–1928). Other prominent figures were the philosopher David Hume (1711–76) and the economist Adam Smith (1728–90).

Many notable achievements resulted from the work of Scottish engineers and inventors. For example, James Watt (1736–1819) revolutionised the steam engine, and John MacAdam (1756–1836) and Thomas Telford (1757–1834) pioneered respectively systems of road building and bridge construction. Alexander Graham Bell (1847–1922) invented the telephone, and John Logie Baird (1888–1946) was the pioneer of television. Scottish scientists have carried out original work of importance in many fields: James Clerk Maxwell (1831–79) propounded the electromagnetic theory of radiation, and Lord Kelvin (1824–1917) founded the modern study of thermodynamics. In medicine John Hunter (1728–93) was the founder of scientific surgery; Sir James Young Simpson (1811–70) was responsible for the introduction and use of chloroform; Sir Alexander Fleming (1881–1955) discovered penicillin; and Marie Stopes (1881–1958) was a pioneer of birth control.

Population

The estimated population of Scotland at the end of June 1991 was 5.1 million (see Table 1). This represented a decrease of some 80,000 since 1981. Over the decade a net migration loss of 107,000 was only partly offset by a natural increase—the excess of births over deaths—of 27,000.

In the last decade the major growth areas in terms of population increase have been Grampian and Highland regions, with increases of 6 and 5 per cent respectively. The largest population fall, of 15 per cent, was recorded in the Shetland Islands, mainly reflecting the loss of oil terminal construction workers temporarily resident in 1981. Other significant decreases were recorded for the Western Isles (7 per cent) and Strathclyde (5 per cent).

Much of the population lives in the central belt, which contains the cities of Glasgow (population 687,590), Edinburgh, the capital (438,780), and Dundee (172,120). The other main city, Aberdeen (213,910), lies north of the central belt. Over the past few decades there has been some movement of population away from the cities to the neighbouring districts and to the five new towns of Cumbernauld, East Kilbride, Glenrothes, Irvine and Livingston, whose combined populations are about a quarter of a million.

The density of population in Scotland is relatively low, with 66 people per square kilometre, compared with 237 in Britain as a whole. It ranges from 3,477 people per square kilometre in Glasgow to eight in the Highland region.

Scottish people in the lowlands have for centuries spoken 'Scots', a dialect derived from the Northumbrian branch of Old English. This has its own recognised literary tradition and has seen a revival in poetry in the twentieth century. Many words and phrases from the Scots tongue are retained in the everyday English which is spoken throughout Scotland. Scots Gaelic, a language of ancient Celtic origin, is spoken by some 80,000 people. The greatest concentration of Gaelic speakers is in the islands of the Hebrides.

Table 1: Estimated Population June 1991

Regions	Population	Sq km	Population density (people per sq km)
Strathclyde	2,296,300	13,529	170
Lothian	750,500	1,756	427
Grampian	514,400	8,707	59
Tayside	391,900	7,502	52
Fife	346,500	1,308	265
Central	272,800	2,627	104
Highland	204,200	25,304	8
Dumfries and Galloway	147,800	6,370	23
Borders	104,100	4,670	22
Islands:			
Western Isles	29,420	2,898	10
Shetland Islands	22,500	1,433	16
Orkney Islands	19,580	976	20
Scotland	**5,100,000**	**77,080**	**66**

Source: General Register Office for Scotland.

Religion

Since 1688 the Protestant Church of Scotland has had the status of national, established church of Scotland. It has complete freedom in all matters of doctrine, order and discipline. Under its presbyterian form of government all ministers have equal status and each of the 1,600 or so churches is governed by its own Kirk Session, consisting of a minister and elders. Above the Kirk Session is the Presbytery, then the General Assembly of the Church of Scotland, consisting of elected ministers and lay elders. This meets annually in Edinburgh for policy and other important discussions under the presidency of an elected moderator, who serves for one year. The Queen is represented at the General Assembly by the Lord High Commissioner. The adult communicant membership of the Church of Scotland is some 770,000.

Training for the ministry is open to men and women, and reflects the high reputation for scholarship which has always been enjoyed by the Church of Scotland. All four older universities (Aberdeen, Edinburgh, Glasgow and St Andrews) offer courses of study leading to the grant of a licence to preach. The Church of Scotland is active in social and educational affairs and has a long tradition of work overseas. It is a strong supporter of Christian unity and is a member of the Council of Churches for Britain and Ireland and the World Council of Churches.

The Roman Catholic Church is the second largest church in Scotland, with a considerable following, especially among people of Irish descent, in Glasgow and the west, but also in some of the remoter parts of the Highlands and Western Isles. It has suffered less than the Protestant church from the decline in church-going during the twentieth century. Other Christian denominations include the Episcopal Church (which follows the doctrine and worship of the Church of England but exists as an independent entity), the Baptist, Congregational and Methodist Churches, and a number of small presbyterian sects.

There are some 40,000 members of ethnic minority groups in Scotland, and their religions—notably Islam, Hinduism, Sikhism and Judaism—are practised, principally in the cities.

Administration

Special arrangements are made for the conduct of Scottish affairs within the British system of government. Because there are certain differences in law and practice between Scotland and the rest of Britain, separate Acts of Parliament for Scotland are enacted when appropriate. All hereditary Scottish peers and peeresses are entitled to sit in the House of Lords, and Scottish constituencies elect 72 Members of Parliament (MPs) to the House of Commons. The general election in April 1992 resulted in the election of 49 Labour MPs, 11 Conservative, 9 Liberal Democrat and 3 Scottish National.

Most purely Scottish business in the House of Commons is conducted in special committees made up predominantly of Scottish MPs. The Scottish Grand Committee, which consists of all 72 Scottish MPs, considers most public Bills concerned exclusively with Scotland which have been referred for debate at Second Reading stage. It also debates financial matters which fall under the competence of the Secretary of State for Scotland and other matters of concern to Scotland. Since 1982 the Scottish Grand Committee has convened a number of times in Edinburgh. There are two Scottish standing committees, whose duties are to examine in detail Bills which are exclusively Scottish. Provision is also made for a Select Committee on Scottish Affairs, consisting of 11 Scottish MPs, to examine the expenditure, administration and policy of The Scottish Office and associated public bodies. Scottish business is debated regularly in both Houses of Parliament, and the

Secretary of State and Scottish ministers answer questions in Parliament on Scottish affairs.

The Secretary of State for Scotland, who is a member of the Cabinet, has ministerial responsibility for most matters affecting Scotland and is head of The Scottish Office. He or she has a major role in the planning and development of the Scottish economy and has important functions relating to industrial development, including responsibility for financial assistance to industry. In carrying out these responsibilities, the Secretary of State has the help of a ministerial team, at present consisting of one Minister of State and three Parliamentary Under-Secretaries of State.

Government Departments

The duties of the Secretary of State are performed mostly through The Scottish Office's five departments (see below), the headquarters of which are in Edinburgh. There are also four smaller departments: the Registers of Scotland Executive Agency, the Scottish Record Office, the General Register Office for Scotland and the Scottish Courts Administration (SCA).

The principal government law officer in Scotland is the Lord Advocate. His responsibilities are performed principally through the two departments shown in Table 3, but he also has certain responsibilities for the work of the SCA.

Most government departments with responsibilities for the whole of the United Kingdom or Great Britain (for example, the Department of Employment and the Inland Revenue) have Scottish headquarters. These are under the charge of a senior officer responsible for the transaction of business in Scotland and for advising on policy affecting Scotland.

Table 2: Functions of Main Scottish Office Departments

The Scottish Office Agriculture and Fisheries Department
Promotion of the agricultural and fishing industries; enforcement of fisheries laws and regulations through the Scottish Fisheries Protection Agency.

The Scottish Office Environment Department
Environment, including environmental protection, nature conservation and the countryside; land use planning; water supplies and sewerage; local government; housing; building control; protection and presentation to the public of historic buildings and ancient monuments through Historic Scotland.

The Scottish Office Education Department
Education; student awards; the arts; libraries, museums and galleries; Gaelic language; sport and recreation.

The Scottish Office Home and Health Department
Central administration of law and order (including police service, criminal justice, legal aid and penal institutions); the National Health Service; fire, home defence and civil emergency services; social work services.

The Scottish Office Industry Department
Industrial and regional economic development matters; co-ordination of Scottish Office European interests; employment; training; energy; tourism; urban regeneration; new towns; roads and certain transport functions.

Central Services
Services to the five Scottish Office departments. These include the Office of the Solicitor to the Secretary of State; the Scottish Office Information Directorate, Personnel Management and Office Management Divisions.

Source: The Scottish Office.

Table 3: Functions of Lord Advocate's Departments

Lord Advocate's Department

Provision of legal advice to the Government on issues affecting Scotland. Responsibility for drafting primary legislation relating wholly or mainly to Scotland and for the adaptation for Scotland of other primary legislation.

Crown Office

Control of all prosecutions in Scotland.

Source: The Scottish Office.

Measures to Improve Government

Under the Next Steps initiative, intended to improve management in the Civil Service and the efficiency and quality of services provided to the public, separate executive agencies are being set up to perform the executive functions of government. By mid-1992 four agencies had been established by The Scottish Office. These are Historic Scotland, the Scottish Fisheries Protection Agency, the Scottish Agricultural Science Agency and Registers of Scotland. Other areas of The Scottish Office are being considered for agency status.

In July 1991 the Government published a White Paper, *The Citizen's Charter: Raising the Standard*,[2] containing over 70 specific measures to raise standards in public service. The Citizen's Charter is intended to raise quality, secure better value and extend accountability in public services. In Scotland four main charters have been issued—the Patient's Charter, the Parents' Charter, the Tenant's Charter and the Justice Charter. The key principles underlying the Citizen's Charter are progressively being applied

[2]Cm 1599. HMSO, £8.50. ISBN 0 10 115992 7.

throughout those organisations which provide services to the public and for which the Secretary of State is responsible.

Expenditure

Expenditure on the programmes for which the Secretary of State is responsible (including that of the Forestry Commission) is forecast to rise from around £11,700 million in 1991–92 to over £12,500 million in 1992–93 (see Table 4). In 1993–94 the resources available for these programmes will be over £13,500 million, 4.5 per cent more than in 1992–93 in real terms—or 2 per cent after allowing for the addition of certain new responsibilities. Three new special initiatives for Scotland were announced in November 1992: a £70 million package of construction-related work; increased resources to address housing problems; and a reduction in 1993–94 of business rates.

Local Government

The Scottish mainland is divided into nine regions: Highland, Grampian, Tayside, Central, Fife, Lothian, Strathclyde, Dumfries and Galloway, and Borders. These are subdivided into 53 districts, each region and district having its own elected council. Three virtually all-purpose authorities serve the islands of Orkney, Shetland and the Western Isles. There is provision for local community councils to be formed, but such councils are not local authorities and have no specific statutory functions.

Each local authority consists of elected councillors presided over by a chairman or woman. The chairmen or women of the district councils of Glasgow, Aberdeen, Edinburgh and Dundee retain the traditional title of Lord Provost. The title of Convener is given

Table 4: Public Expenditure within the Responsibility of the Secretary of State for Scotland

£ million

	1992–93 (estimated outturn)	1993–94 (plans)
Agriculture, fisheries and food	331	441
Industry, energy, trade and employment	544	530
Roads and transport	431	406
Housing	668	664
Other environmental services	387	361
Law, order and protective services	406	448
Education	636	1,167
Arts and libraries	49	54
Health	3,643	3,766
Social work services	62	63
Other public services	180	185
Total	**7,337**	**8,085**
Grants from the European Regional Development Fund	0	120
Central government support to local authorities' current expenditure	5,203	5,207
Nationalised industries' financing limits	32	35
Total expenditure within the Secretary of State's responsibility	**12,571**	**13,446**
Forestry Commission*	99	94
Total Scotland	12,670	12,540

Source: The Scottish Office

Notes:
1. Differences between totals and the sums of their component parts are due to rounding.
2. Central government support to local authorities comprises revenue support grant, grants for specific purposes, and income from non-domestic rates.
3. Comparisons between 1992–93 are affected by transfers of responsibility in respect of education and care in the community.
4. For 1992–93 expenditure financed by grants from the European Regional Development Fund was included in the relevant programme total.

*The inclusion of the Forestry Commission in the expenditure for Scotland reflects the Secretary of State for Scotland's lead role in forestry matters.

to the chairmen or women of the regional councils and some district councils, and the title of Provost is used in some other districts. Local authority areas vary greatly in population, from 10,000 in the smallest districts to nearly 2.3 million in Strathclyde (see Table 1).

Regional authorities are responsible for strategic planning functions and other major services, such as transport, water supply and sewerage, education, social work services, the police, and fire services.

District authorities are generally responsible for housing and for matters such as local planning, leisure and recreation, libraries and environmental health. The three islands authorities have statutory responsibility for almost the whole range of local government functions. However, they participate in wider-scale administrative arrangements for their police and fire services and rely on the mainland for help in the more specialised aspects of education and social work.

At the end of 1990 the Government began a wide-ranging review of the structure and internal management of local government. Arising from that review, the Secretary of State for Scotland issued a consultation paper in June 1991 (see Further Reading, p. 95) which sought views on a proposal to move to single-tier local authorities throughout Scotland to replace the existing two-tier structure. A second, more detailed consultation paper on the subject was issued in October 1992, inviting views on the form that a single-tier structure would take. Comments are being invited by 29 January 1993 and the Government expects to issue a White Paper in summer 1993.

At present, local authorities derive a significant part of their revenue from the levying and collection of the community charge, a local tax payable at a flat rate by each resident. The business sector also pays a local tax called the non-domestic rates. This is geared to the rateable value of the property occupied by business. The non-domestic rate is levied by local government but set up by central government, with annual increases being limited to the rate of inflation. Central government also pays revenue support grant to local authorities. Government grants are also paid towards expenditure for particular purposes, such as tackling urban deprivation. In addition, annual subsidies are paid for local authority housing.

From April 1993 a new form of taxation—the council tax—will replace the community charge. The tax will be based on the market value of property and will take account of the number of people in each household. It will be collected from nearly all domestic households.

The Convention of Scottish Local Authorities represents the interests of all local authorities in discussions and consultations with central government departments. A Scottish Commissioner for Local Administration (Local Government Ombudsman) is responsible for investigating citizens' complaints of injustice caused by maladministration.

The Legal System

Scotland has its own legal system, which differs considerably in law, organisation and practice from that followed in the rest of Britain. However, a large volume of modern legislation applies throughout Britain.

The main sources of law are common law, government legislation and European Community law. Common law is the ancient law of the land drawn from custom and interpreted by judges. This forms the basis of the law except when superceded by legislation. European Community law is confined mainly to economic and social matters, and where applicable takes precedence over domestic law.

Courts

The judiciary, as in the rest of Britain, is independent and is not subject to ministerial direction or control.

The Supreme Courts are the High Court of Justiciary for criminal cases and the Court of Session for civil cases. Both sit in Edinburgh, but the High Court of Justiciary also sits in other major towns and cities. The High Court tries the most serious crimes and has exclusive jurisdiction in cases involving murder, treason and rape.

Below the Supreme Courts are 49 Sheriff Courts, organised into six sheriffdoms, each of which is headed by a sheriff principal. The Sheriff Courts deal with the less serious criminal cases and with civil cases. A further tier of district courts, administered by local authorities and usually presided over by lay justices of the peace, deals with minor offences.

Criminal Prosecution

All criminal cases in the High Court of Justiciary and the more serious ones in the Sheriff Courts are tried by a judge and jury. Less serious cases in the Sheriff Courts and all cases in the district courts are tried solely by a judge.

A jury is independent of the judiciary, and consists of 15 people. Potential jurors are put on a panel before the start of a trial, and the prosecution or defence may challenge up to three jurors without giving reason for doing so.

The jury's verdict may be 'guilty', 'not guilty' or 'not proven', and the accused is acquitted if either of the last two verdicts is given. A verdict of 'guilty' can be reached if at least eight members are in favour but, as a general rule, no one may be convicted without corroborated evidence from at least two sources.

As in the rest of Britain, if the jury acquits the defendant, the prosecution has no right of appeal and the defendant cannot be tried again for the same offence. The defendant, however, has a right of appeal to the appropriate court if found guilty.

Appeals in all criminal cases are heard by the Court of Criminal Appeal of the High Court of Justiciary. In civil cases appeals are heard by the Inner House of the Court of Session, from which there is a right of appeal to the House of Lords. An appeal may be brought by the accused against conviction, or sentence, or both. The Court may authorise a retrial if it sets aside a conviction.

Prosecutions of children in the criminal courts are rare. Instead, children under 16—and, in some cases, young people between 16 and 18—who have committed an offence or are considered to be in need of care and protection can be brought before a children's hearing, in which a panel comprising three members of the local community decides on appropriate action. This hearing determines in an informal setting whether compulsory measures of care are required and, if so, the form that they should take. Any offender between the ages of 16 and 21 who is given a custodial sentence by a court is placed in a young offender institution.

The Lord Advocate is responsible for prosecutions in the High Court of Justiciary, Sheriff Courts and district courts. Prosecutions are prepared by procurators fiscal, the police being responsible for investigating crimes and reporting to the fiscal. When dealing with minor crime, the procurator fiscal increasingly makes use of alternatives to prosecution, such as formal warnings and fixed penalties.

Civil Courts

The Civil Courts are the Court of Session and the Sheriff Courts. Sheriff Courts have jurisdiction over most civil litigation and have exclusive jurisdiction over cases with a value not exceeding £1,500. Appeals may be made to the sheriff principal or directly to the Court of Session in 'ordinary causes'. In 'summary causes' (generally cases where the value of the claim is between £750 and £1,500), an appeal may be made to the sheriff principal on a point of law and thereafter to the Court of Session only if the sheriff principal certifies the case as suitable. In small claims cases (those for under £750) an appeal is only possible to the sheriff principal on a point of law. The Court of Session is divided into the Outer House, a court of first instance, and the Inner House, mainly an appeal court.

The Scottish Land Court deals exclusively with matters concerning agriculture. Its judicial head has the status and tenure of a judge of the Court of Session and its other members are lay specialists.

Treatment of Offenders

The Scottish Office Home and Health Department administers prisons and young offender institutions. In 1991 there were 19 establishments, including three young offender institutions for young people aged between 16 and 21. After a decline in recent years in inmate numbers from around 5,300 in the mid-1980s to about 4,800 in 1991, totals again rose in the first half of 1992, to some 5,300. There are also a range of alternatives to custody including probation orders, community service orders and supervised attendance orders.

Remission of part of the sentence for good behaviour, release on parole and supervision on release are available for offenders. The release of prisoners serving life sentences is at the discretion of the Secretary of State for Scotland, subject to a favourable recommendation by the relevant parole board and after consultation with the judiciary.

Police Service

Overall responsibility for the police rests with the Secretary of State for Scotland, who is assisted by the Chief Inspector of Constabulary for Scotland. There are eight police forces, based on local government regions and islands, with a total strength of 14,200 (excluding civilian staff). Each force is maintained by a police authority, drawn from local councillors, and is headed by a chief constable, who is responsible for the direction and control of the force. A Scottish Crime Squad provides a common service to assist police forces in the investigation and prevention of major crime.

The police may detain and question a suspect for up to six hours. After this period the person must either be released or charged. Anyone accused of a crime, except murder or treason, is entitled to apply for release on bail. Even in cases of murder or treason, bail may be granted at the discretion of the Lord Advocate or a quorum of the High Court.

Administration of the Law

The Secretary of State for Scotland recommends the appointment of most judges and is responsible for the composition, staffing, accommodation and financing of the Supreme and Sheriff Courts. District courts are staffed and administered by the district and islands local authorities.

The Secretary of State is also responsible for Scottish criminal law, crime prevention, the police, the penal system and legal aid. The Lord Advocate and the Solicitor General for Scotland are the chief legal advisers to the Government on Scottish questions and the principal representatives of the Crown for the purpose of litigation in Scotland. Both are government ministers. The law is kept under review by the Scottish Law Commission, which reports annually to the Lord Advocate.

The Economy

The present pattern of Scotland's economy is broadly similar to that of Britain as a whole. Scotland's gross domestic product (GDP) forms about 8 per cent of the total for Britain and in 1990 amounted to some £38,700 million, representing £7,600 per head of the population. Economic growth in Scotland has generally been greater recently than in the rest of Britain. The Scottish economy, like other regional economies in Britain, experienced a reduction in overall economic activity in 1991. The effects of the recession have been less pronounced though than in other parts of Britain, with the decline in GDP expected to be less than that recorded in Britain as a whole.

One of the most significant long-term economic developments has been the dramatic growth of oil-related industries, following the discovery in the late 1960s of oil, and to a lesser extent gas, under the North Sea. This brought about a considerable expansion in the economy generally, with wider employment opportunities and a rise in average earnings and standards of living. It is estimated that about 100,000 jobs (in a labour force of about 2.3 million in Scotland) have been created directly or indirectly in the oil, gas and related industries. In response to the offshore industry, communications, both domestic and international, have improved, particularly in the north and north east.

As traditional, heavy industries, such as coal, steel and ship-building, have declined, there has been growth in industries such as chemicals, electronic engineering, food, drink and tobacco, and lighter forms of mechanical and instrument engineering. Scotland now has one of the biggest concentrations of the electronics industry in Western Europe, with around 210 plants employing some 47,000 workers.

At the same time there has been a marked expansion in the services sector of the economy, including insurance, banking, finance, franchising, distribution, and hotels and catering, which are benefiting from a thriving tourist industry. Between 1982 and 1992 the number of employees in service industries rose by 200,000 (16 per cent) to over 1.4 million. In 1992 about 72 per cent of the labour force was employed in the services sector, compared with 54 per cent in 1974, whereas manufacturing accounted for less than 19 per cent in 1992, compared with 33 per cent in 1974. Tourism and leisure industries directly provide over 155,000 jobs—8 per cent of Scottish employment.

Overseas companies, particularly from the United States and Japan, have played an important role in the transformation of the Scottish economy. In addition, Britain's membership of the European Community has influenced the location in Scotland of many undertakings with headquarters in other European countries. In 1990 it was estimated that overseas-owned companies accounted for 24 per cent of manufacturing employment in Scotland, employing about 86,000 people. Of the 389 overseas-owned manufacturing plants, about one-half were owned by United States firms and nearly a quarter were engaged in the electrical and instrument engineering sector. Since 1981 there has been £4,200 million of overseas investment in Scotland.

In 1991–92 Locate in Scotland and The Scottish Office Industry Department secured planned inward investment of £381 million and the creation and safeguarding of 6,000 jobs. The largest investment was a £180 million international medical complex being built at Clydebank for Health Care International; this is the biggest single inward investment in Scotland to date.

The greater part of Scottish industry is located in the central belt, an area bounded by Ayr and Greenock in the west and Edinburgh and Dundee in the east. However, North Sea oil developments have led to a considerable industrial expansion in the north east and, to a lesser extent, in some other areas of the country.

Employment

Total employment in Scotland, as measured by the civilian workforce in employment, was provisionally estimated at 2.26 million in June 1992, 7 per cent more than in 1982, although slightly below the level of June 1991. Employment in services continues to grow, whereas employment in manufacturing and construction has declined. As elsewhere in Britain, self-employment is becoming more important. Between June 1982 and June 1991 self-employment increased by 55 per cent to 254,000, representing 11.1 per cent of the workforce in employment, although there was a decline to 234,000 by June 1992.

Unemployment fell substantially in the second half of the 1980s, from around 14 per cent in 1986 to 8 per cent in late 1990. As in the rest of Britain, unemployment in the early 1990s has increased in Scotland, but at a lower rate than elsewhere. By September 1992 unemployment as a percentage of the workforce, on a seasonally adjusted basis, was provisionally estimated at 9.7 per cent, slightly below that for Britain as a whole (10.1 per cent).

Several schemes, financed by the Government, have been introduced since the mid-1970s to alleviate the effects of unemployment, especially among young people and the long-term unemployed. In September 1992 some 35,800 people were participating in Youth Training, which gives young people who choose not to stay on in full-time education and who are not already employed the opportunity of a broad-based vocational education leading to a vocational qualification or a credit towards one. Training credits, which operate within the broad framework of Youth Training, give young people who have left full-time education to join the labour market an entitlement to train to approved standards. Pilot projects were started by one Local Enterprise Company (see p. 34) in April 1991 and two more will start offering credits in April 1993. Employment Training provides a flexible and individually adapted training programme to help longer-term unemployed people acquire the skills needed for work, including for many the chance to acquire an appropriate qualification or credit towards one.

Statistics for employment, including an analysis of the main sectors, are given in Table 5.

Economic Development

Responsibility for co-ordinating economic development measures rests with The Scottish Office Industry Department, which also oversees their implementation and administers selective financial assistance under the Industrial Development Act 1982. There is also an advisory and consultative Scottish Economic Council, whose members are drawn from industry, commerce, trade unions, local authorities, agriculture and the universities, and which meets under the chairmanship of the Secretary of State for Scotland.

Since the 1930s the Scottish economy has benefited substantially from government financial aid schemes aimed at attracting new employment to areas of Britain suffering from industrial decline and unemployment. There are two types of

Table 5: Employment

Thousands

	1982	1987	June 1990	1991	1992
Employment					
Self-employed	164	194	234	254	234*
Employees in employment	1,950	1,878	1,979	1,984	1,983*
Work-related government training	–	34	56	46	43*
Total workforce in employment	**2,114**	**2,106**	**2,269**	**2,284**	**2,260***
Employees in employment by sector					
Agriculture, forestry and fishing	39	31	30	28	27
Energy and water supply	72	55	59	59	57
Manufacturing	477	406	399	385	368
of which					
Metal manufacturing and chemicals	*63*	*47*	*43*	*38*	*36*
Metal goods, engineering and vehicles	*204*	*165*	*165*	*153*	*147*
Other manufacturing	*209*	*195*	*191*	*194*	*185*
Construction	135	124	131	117	103
Services	1,228	1,261	1,359	1,394	1,428
of which					
Distribution, hotels and catering, repairs	*384*	*366*	*410*	*415*	*419*
Transport and communications	*124*	*113*	*112*	*111*	*109*
Banking, insurance and finance	*135*	*159*	*191*	*205*	*223*
Other services	*585*	*623*	*649*	*662*	*676*

Source: The Scottish Office Industry Department.

*Provisional figures.

Note: Differences between totals and the sum of their component parts are due to rounding.

Assisted Area[3] in Scotland—Development Areas and Intermediate Areas, with the former attracting higher levels of assistance. The Assisted Areas include a considerable part of the Strathclyde region, the Dundee/Arbroath area in Tayside, all the Scottish new towns, most of the Highlands and Islands, and a number of areas in central and south-west Scotland.

Current measures are designed to encourage the development of a self-sustaining enterprise economy and the growth of employment in viable enterprises. They include regional assistance and grants to Scottish Enterprise and Highlands and Islands Enterprise (see below). Expenditure on regional assistance to Scottish industry in 1991-92 amounted to £78 million including £64 million of Regional Selective Assistance (RSA). New offers of RSA in 1991-92 were expected to create 6,500 jobs and safeguard 1,900.

RSA—the principal form of regional assistance—is a discretionary scheme which provides grant assistance to companies in the Assisted Areas for investment projects which involve expansion, modernisation or rationalisation and which create or safeguard jobs. In addition, the Regional Enterprise Grant (REG) scheme provides a simplified form of support for investment and innovation projects being undertaken by small businesses. The Investment Grant element of REG is available to businesses in Development Areas and in part of Fife.

Support for industrial research and development, which is available throughout Scotland, is being channelled increasingly into the development and industrial application of advanced technologies. A significant source of financial aid for economic growth is the various European Community funds.[4]

[3]A review of the Assisted Areas in Britain is in progress.
[4]For further details see *Britain in the European Community* (Aspects of Britain: HMSO 1992).

In the private sector, economic development is promoted by the Scottish Council Development and Industry, with 1,250 members. It is supported by voluntary subscription and is widely representative of industry and commerce, trade unions and professional associations, local authorities, educational establishments and the financial services sector. The Council's current activities fall into three main areas: public policy, business and trade development, and manpower and education. As part of its trade development programme, for example, eight overseas trade missions were arranged, with 118 companies participating, in the year ended September 1992. The Council also commissions economic reports and studies, organises conferences, and provides information and consultancy services.

Enterprise

Changes to the mechanism for government support for enterprise and training in Scotland were outlined in a White Paper in 1988—*Scottish Enterprise: A New Approach to Training and Enterprise Creation* (see Further Reading)—and implemented under the Enterprise and New Towns (Scotland) Act 1990. Under the Act, the training, enterprise and environmental improvement activities administered by the then Scottish Development Agency and those in Scotland of the Training Agency were brought together, with similar but separate arrangements for the Highlands and Islands. Two new bodies—Scottish Enterprise and its counterpart, Highlands and Islands Enterprise—have succeeded the Scottish Development Agency, the former Highlands and Islands Development Board and the Training Agency in Scotland. The main functions of the new bodies are to further the development of Scotland's economy, enhance the skills of the workforce, stimulate industrial efficiency and competitiveness, promote self-employment and improve the environment. These functions are largely contracted out to a network of 22 Local Enterprise Companies (LECs) which carry out assessments of the enterprise and skills of their local areas and arrange the provision of training and business support (see below).

Scottish Enterprise and Highlands and Islands Enterprise encourage investment in the development of skills throughout the workforce and invest directly in training, particularly for school-leavers and the long-term unemployed. They offer a range of advisory and training services to businesses to enhance the expertise of their employees. They also seek to ensure that investment funding for businesses in the private sector is adequate. Where necessary, they contribute financially to such provision. They also remove obstacles to economic development through the treatment of derelict land and by contributing to the improvement of the infrastructure of towns and cities.

Scottish Enterprise

Resources available to the Scottish Enterprise network in 1992–93 amount to some £460 million. Scottish Enterprise is the main agency for handling economic development projects and programmes in lowland Scotland.

Scottish Enterprise is encouraging enterprise development in its area and about £90 million is allocated for this purpose in 1992–93. Two new initiatives have been established to help companies in Scotland develop their exporting activity. In December 1991 Scottish Enterprise combined forces with the Exports Division of The Scottish Office to form Scottish Trade International, which promotes Scottish goods and services overseas and helps Scottish companies to understand export markets, recognise opportunities, and to promote their products appropriately and effectively. Another initiative is Scotland Europa, launched in May 1992, which promotes Scottish interests in Brussels. It provides research and analysis services in Brussels for Scottish companies, organisations and other bodies.

Environmental improvement is a significant aspect of Scottish Enterprise's activities, with a budget allocation of £84 million in 1992–93. Additional resources are being concentrated for a special programme in Lanarkshire, following the announcement of the closure in mid-1992 of the steelworks at Ravenscraig.

Highlands and Islands Enterprise

Highlands and Islands Enterprise replaced the former Highlands and Islands Development Board, which had been set up in 1965 with the broad aim of improving economic and social conditions in the Highlands and Islands. It has similar responsibilities to those of Scottish Enterprise, but with an additional responsibility for social development. This latter function is undertaken so as to maintain self-sustaining local economies. Most of its functions are carried out under contract by the ten LECs which operate in its area.

In 1992-93 its available resources amount to over £78 million, of which £47.5 million are connected with enterprise development.

Local Enterprise Companies

The network of 22 LECs in Scotland is now fully operational. They have wider responsibilities than their equivalent bodies in England and Wales, the Training and Enterprise Councils (TECs), as they also cover economic development and environmental improvement. LECs operate the same programmes as the TECs. These include Youth Training and Employment Training (see p. 28).

Locate in Scotland

Locate in Scotland was set up in 1981. It is a joint operation between The Scottish Office Industry Department and Scottish Enterprise, working closely with Highlands and Islands Enterprise. It has four main purposes:

—to market Scotland overseas as a location for investment;

—to advise potential investors;

—to negotiate an appropriate development package; and

—to provide support to investing companies after the investment has been made.

Enterprise Zones

Among major schemes of economic regeneration being implemented with the aid of public funds are three enterprise zones,[5] at Inverclyde, Tayside (Arbroath and Dundee), and the Invergordon area of the Highland region. In each of the zones there has been a significant increase in economic activity, in terms of land developed, number of firms, and employment. In 1992, following the announcement of the closure of the Ravenscraig steelworks, the Government announced its intention to designate an enterprise zone in Lanarkshire. This is expected to create some 8,700 jobs in the next ten years.

[5]Enterprise zones are areas in which financial and other incentives are provided to encourage the establishment of industry. The incentives include exemption from the non-domestic rates, 100 per cent allowance against national taxes for capital expenditure on industrial and commercial buildings and a much simplified planning procedure.

Manufacturing, Construction and Services

Engineering and Electronics

Engineering remains a major industry in Scotland, employing about 73 per cent of the total manufacturing workforce. The most rapidly expanding sector is that of electronics, which accounts for 20 per cent of Scotland's manufacturing output and investment. In recent years many of the world's leading electronics firms have set up plants in Scotland.

The success of the oil industry has triggered a revival in heavy engineering, with the manufacture of such items as pumps, valves, process plant and steelwork. The engineering sector has attracted several overseas companies, such as Honeywell of the United States and Volvo Trucks of Sweden. In addition, Scottish firms have had considerable success in competing for overseas engineering contracts.

The output of the Scottish electronics industry grew by 14 per cent a year between 1980 and 1990. The most rapid growth, of 30 per cent a year, was experienced in electronic data-processing equipment (mainly computers and computer control devices). Scotland accounts for over 50 per cent of Britain's output of integrated circuits and over 10 per cent of European output. Total Scottish electronics industry sales were estimated at £4,908 million in 1989, representing 20 per cent of the total British industry sales. By mid-1990 some 46,500 workers were employed in the industry, which accounted for about 13 per cent of total Scottish manufacturing employment. The industry in Scotland is becoming much more skill-intensive.

There has been considerable investment, especially in and around the new towns, by overseas electronics companies, mainly from the United States and Japan. For example, IBM makes its personal computers for European and other international markets at Greenock; Mitsubishi Electric makes video recorders in Livingston; and the Victor Company of Japan (JVC) established its European manufacturing plant at East Kilbride. In 1992 Motorola announced its intention to invest £40 million at its microchip design and production plant at East Kilbride, creating 150 new jobs and raising the company's workforce there to nearly 2,000.

Scottish Enterprise encourages the commercial application of research and technical services developed at Scottish universities and other institutions. Strong links have been established between electronics companies and the universities of Heriot-Watt (Edinburgh) and Strathclyde (Glasgow). Furthermore, a number of science parks[6] have been founded to bridge the gap between research at universities and its practical application in industry. The Riccarton Research Park, established in 1972 next to Heriot-Watt University, was one of the first science parks in Britain. At the West of Scotland Science Park, which was constructed in 1983 as a joint initiative between the Universities of Glasgow and Strathclyde, important research on pharmaceutical products and biotechnology is carried out. The science park at Aberdeen University opened in 1987 and provides accommodation and

---

[6]Science parks are sites, usually near universities, containing science-based industries and designed to facilitate commercial developments in advanced technology through collaboration between university and industrial scientists and technologists.

support for the research and development activity of companies in the oil service and supply industry.

Shipbuilding and Aerospace

The shipbuilding industry in Scotland as elsewhere has suffered a serious decline, but recent reorganisation and modernisation of the shipyards have enabled the remaining yards to win some important contracts. Expertise gained in the construction of vessels and structures connected with the offshore oil industry—for example, drilling rigs—has led to a number of export orders.

Aerospace engine manufacture and repair servicing are carried out at Prestwick airport by the firm of Ryder International. Also at Prestwick, British Aerospace operates the assembly line for the commuter liner Jetstream 31, for which orders or options of 400 have been placed since its first flight in 1982, and the Jetstream 41, of which 25 have been ordered.

Textiles

Scotland is noted for high-quality tweeds and knitwear produced mainly in the small Borders towns of Galashiels, Hawick and Selkirk and from the island groups of the Hebrides, Orkney and Shetland, where Harris tweed and Shetland knitwear are made. Tweeds, including tartan materials, knitted goods and top-quality leather clothing, have a wide export market. Scotland is Britain's main production centre of heavyweight canvas for sail-cloth, tents, awnings and tarpaulins.

Chemicals

A diversified chemicals industry produces petrochemicals, pharmaceuticals, plastics, dyestuffs, fertilisers and explosives.

Expansion has taken place in a number of products, notably pharmaceuticals related to the developing health care industry. A large number of multinational companies are based in Scotland, including Roche, Glaxo and SmithKline Beecham.

Fertilisers are manufactured in the Lothian region and in the north east, and paintworks and certain other chemical manufacturing firms are located in Glasgow. Among major British chemical firms represented in Scotland are British Petroleum (BP) and Imperial Chemical Industries (ICI), both with operations in the large-scale petrochemical complex at Grangemouth and elsewhere in the country. There are also petrochemical operations at Mossmorran and Kinnell.

Construction

The construction industry has been affected by changing demand from the offshore oil industry, for which it builds roads, pipelines, storage tanks, plant, harbour extensions, warehouses, factories, offices and housing. Following a decline in demand after the first phase of oil development, output in the construction industry then improved again. In 1990 output rose by 13 per cent to £4,247 million: £731 million of new housing, £1,603 million of other new work and £1,913 million of repairs and maintenance.

Other Manufacturing

The food and drink industries employ more than 65,000 people, many of whom are based in the smaller towns and rural areas. Bread and confectionery, bacon curing, meat and fish products, brewing, malting and whisky distilling are the principal activities, with whisky as the most important single product. Whisky exports represented about one-fifth of Scotland's overseas exports in 1990, when they totalled £1,700 million. There are 114 whisky distilleries, most of which are in the north east, while Glasgow is the centre for blending and bottling. The principal breweries are in Edinburgh and Alloa. Paisley and Greenock specialise in sugar refining, Dundee in chocolate and sweet manufacture, and Edinburgh in biscuit manufacture. As well as the traditional products associated with Scotland, such as salmon, high-quality beef, shortbread and whisky, the food and drinks industry includes speciality products, such as flavoured cheeses, mineral water and shellfish.

In recent years companies have been concentrating on developing high-quality products, particularly pre-packed and cooked foodstuffs. Various quality assurance schemes have been developed in Scotland to assure consumers that appropriate care and attention throughout the food chain have gone into the preparation of products.

Edinburgh is one of the major centres in Britain for fine printing and book-binding. Besides high-quality papers and boards, many specialised papers are produced in Scotland.

A number of smaller companies manufacture bricks, pottery, glass, cement, rubber goods and sports equipment.

Tourism

Tourism remains an important sector of the economy. In 1991, 9.8 million visitors spent some £1,740 million in Scotland. Around 1.6 million came from overseas and accounted for £550 million of the tourist expenditure. Tourist-related activities are estimated to account for over 155,000 jobs.

The industry ranges from the small family-run business to the large multinational company, and includes activities such as entertainment, provision of accommodation, transport and retailing. It receives support from the Scottish Tourist Board (STB), Scottish Enterprise, Highlands and Islands Enterprise and local authorities. Good progress has been made in providing and improving amenities and facilities. To promote further improvements, the STB has introduced a comprehensive classification and grading scheme for accommodation.

The rest of Britain is the most significant source of visitors to Scotland. Many people visit the country for short-break and off-peak holidays. The British Tourist Authority and the STB promote Scotland as a tourist destination to potential overseas visitors, particularly in North America, the rest of Europe and Japan. In addition, promotional schemes are undertaken by a network of local area tourist boards to attract visitors to particular parts of the country.

The Financial Sector

The financial services industry is of growing importance to the Scottish economy, accounting for some 15 per cent of GDP. Employment is over 200,000, around 10 per cent of the workforce, and has grown by more than 25 per cent in the last six years. Scotland's financial institutions have a high reputation internationally. In a range of services—such as investment trusts, branch banking and unit trusts—Scotland has been a pioneer. For example, the Scottish-based clearing banks, which employ over 42,000 people, are well known for innovation, having pioneered cash dispensers and electronic home banking. About one-third of all investment funds in Britain are managed from Scotland, which is also a base for a large number of insurance companies. The nine Scottish life assurance offices account for over 20 per cent of the British markets, with funds in excess of £60,000 million.

Edinburgh is regarded as the country's financial centre, and the headquarters of many financial institutions are located there. Glasgow also has important commercial and banking facilities.

Three of the four Scottish-based clearing banks are long established: the Bank of Scotland, founded in 1695; the Royal Bank of Scotland, founded in 1727; and the Clydesdale Bank, founded in 1838. While forming an integral part of the British monetary system, these banks have full independence and have limited rights to issue their own banknotes, which are accepted by banks throughout Britain. The Scottish banks have offices in London and are also represented overseas, particularly in the United States and the Far East. The Royal Bank of Scotland operates throughout Britain.

The greatly increased demand for capital generated by offshore oil exploration and exploitation provided a new opportunity for Scottish financial institutions and led to the establishment of several merchant banks. Both they and the clearing banks have invested substantially in North Sea oil and gas and have collaborated in ventures related to oil development.

The London Stock Exchange has an administrative centre in Glasgow.

Energy and Water Resources

Scotland has a wide range of energy resources: coal, nuclear, hydro-electric power, oil and gas. The potential for other renewable resources, such as wind power, is being considered.

Oil

Since the Montrose oilfield was discovered in 1969, over 50 offshore fields have come into production in the United Kingdom Continental Shelf. At the end of 1991, 46 offshore fields were in production, and during 1991, 17 oil and condensate development plans were approved. The first oil was brought ashore in 1975, when production started in the Argyll field. In 1985 Britain's oil production reached a peak of 127.5 million tonnes, when it exceeded consumption by 78 million tonnes. By 1991 production had decreased to 91.3 million tonnes and consumption increased to 82.8 million tonnes. Some 33,200 people were employed offshore in September 1991, compared with some 28,200 people in September 1987. In 1991 the Government awarded exploration licences for 74 blocks in the twelfth exploration round after receiving the highest number of applications in ten years.

The trend in offshore oil and gas developments is towards exploitation of smaller reservoirs. This trend has been made more economic by scientific and technological advances, such as subsea production systems.

Some 1,878 km (1,174 miles) of major submarine pipeline bring oil ashore from the North Sea oilfields. The oil is then transported from the shore terminals either by tanker or by land pipeline. The main submarine terminals are at Sullom Voe in Shetland, Flotta in Orkney, Nigg on the Cromarty Firth and Cruden Bay in Grampian. Pipelines connect Cruden Bay with Grangemouth on the Forth, where there is a large oil refinery forming part of the complex operated by BP.

On the largest oilfields production is controlled from steel or concrete platforms built to withstand severe weather and heavy seas. More than half the platforms have been built by Scottish construction firms, which have carried out extensive pioneering work in this field. Onshore services and supply facilities have been developed rapidly to meet the needs of the oil industry, notably at Aberdeen but also at the Cromarty Firth, the Orkney and Shetland Islands, Peterhead, Montrose and Dundee. The Department of Trade and Industry's Offshore Supplies Office, which has its headquarters in Glasgow, promotes fair commercial opportunity for British firms in all oil and gas markets. It also supports the development of the latest technology, promotes British exports and provides the secretariat for the Offshore Industry Advisory Board. The Board, chaired by a Department of Trade and Industry energy minister, is the principal source of high-level co-ordinated advice on the development of strategy for Britain's offshore supplies industry.

Gas

Natural gas from the North Sea has progressively replaced town gas in the public supply in Scotland since 1970. Much of it comes from the Frigg natural gas field, and an increasing quantity is being produced in association with oil from North Sea oilfields. Two 362-km (225-mile) underwater pipelines have been laid between the Frigg field and St Fergus (Grampian), where there is a major gas terminal. Another pipeline, 452 km (281 miles) long, connects the Brent field with St Fergus. Gas is brought south by land pipeline to link up with the grid system operated by British Gas. A demonstration coal gasification plant has been built by British Gas at its Westfield Development Centre in Fife.

Coal

Although the coal industry was traditionally of great importance to the Scottish economy, output has been falling in recent years and production is now concentrated in one deep mine and a number of opencast sites in the coalfields of the Strathclyde, Central, Lothian and Fife regions, in the central belt. Output of deep-mined and opencast coal here amounts to some 7 million tonnes annually, more than half of which is used by electricity generating stations. Britain's largest power station, at Longannet in Fife, is served by one of the most modern coalmining complexes in Europe.

Electricity

Restructuring of the electricity supply industry in Scotland in 1990–91 involved privatisation of the two former nationalised boards and the creation of three companies. Two of these, Scottish Power plc and Scottish Hydro-Electric plc, generate, transmit, distribute and supply electricity. They are also contracted to buy all the electricity output from Scottish Nuclear Ltd, which operates two nuclear power stations. Total generating capacity is around 9,500 megawatts (MW) and electricity is supplied to 2.5 million customers.

In 1991–92 Scottish Nuclear's 1,040-MW advanced gas-cooled reactor (AGR) at Hunterston (Strathclyde) and its 1,400-

MW AGR at Torness (Lothian) supplied about 40 per cent of the electricity generated in Scotland. The power stations operated by Scottish Power and Scottish Hydro-Electric provided the balance. Scottish Power has 15 power stations and in 1991–92 its three coal-fired stations produced 50 per cent of the electricity supplied in its area. Hydro-Electric has 59 stations (mostly hydro, but one major oil/gas station), and in 1991–92 they produced 62 per cent of the electricity supplied in its area. Hydro-electric capacity includes major pumped storage schemes at Cruachan on Loch Awe (operated by Scottish Power) and at Foyers on Loch Ness.

Transmission lines linking the Scottish and English grid systems enable cross-border trading. This interconnector is run jointly by Scottish Power and the National Grid Company in England. Scottish Power and Northern Ireland Electricity have agreed in principle to construct a 250-MW interconnector between Scotland and Northern Ireland, to come into operation in 1996.

Energy Efficiency

The Scottish Energy Efficiency Office is one of the 11 regional energy efficiency offices in Britain. It is responsible for promoting energy efficiency in Scotland and is aiming to reduce the use of energy, both to cut costs and to help the environment.

Renewable Sources of Energy

In addition to hydro power from the two public electricity suppliers, and a number of smaller operators, there are other projects in Scotland which use renewable sources.

Wind Power

Britain's largest and most powerful wind power generator was built at Burgar Hill by the Wind Energy Group, with financial support from Scottish Hydro-Electric and the Department of Energy. Inaugurated in 1987, it has a generating capacity of 3 MW and operates in wind speeds of 7 m a second (16 mph) and above. It is capable of generating enough power for over 2,000 homes. Two other generators on the same site, with a capacity of 250 kilowatts (kW) and 300 kW, have produced electricity for the local grid since 1983.

A 750-kW wind turbine has been installed at Susetter Hill in the Shetland Islands, with financial support from the European Community's wind energy demonstration programme. In 1991 the National Wind Turbine Centre, part of the National Engineering Laboratory's Energy and Environment Centre, was opened at East Kilbride. Two wind turbines, each with an output capacity of 300 kW, have been inaugurated on the site.

Wave Energy

In 1991 Britain's first pilot shoreline wave energy device, the world's most technically advanced, was inaugurated on the island of Islay in the Inner Hebrides. It delivers up to 75 kW to the local grid.

Waves entering a natural rock gulley on the island are channelled into a water column, compressing and expanding air as the water column rises and falls. Air movement drives a turbine, which in turn drives an electrical generator.

Water Supply

Scotland has an extensive supply of unspoiled water from upland sources. An average of 2,301 megalitres a day was supplied in 1990–91. Responsibility for public water supply, sewerage and sewage disposal rests with the nine regional and three islands councils. In addition, the Central Scotland Water Development Board is responsible for developing new sources of water for the regional councils in central Scotland. Charges for water vary according to the type of consumer. Domestic consumers pay community water charges, while non-domestic consumers pay non-domestic water rates or metered charges. Charges and rates are decided by each authority. With the planned changes in local government (see p. 18), a new structure for water and sewerage services will be needed, and consultations about this will be held in parallel with those on local government reform.

Supplies are drawn almost entirely from upland surface sources, such as natural lochs, reservoirs and rivers. Only a small proportion comes from underground sources. Responsibility for promoting the conservation of water resources and for the provision by water authorities of adequate water supplies rests with the Secretary of State for Scotland, who also has a duty, exercised through independent river purification authorities, to promote the cleanliness of rivers and other inland and tidal waters.

Agriculture, Forestry and Fishing

Agriculture

Some 79 per cent of the total land area of Scotland is devoted to agriculture. Of this approximately one-sixth is arable, the remainder being mostly rough grazing. Hill and upland farms account for about two-thirds of the agricultural area. The hill farms supply young stock for fattening in the richer pastures of the lowlands, and the lowland farms provide winter feed for the hill farms. Dairying is concentrated in the south west, where rainfall is relatively high, and in parts of central and north-east Scotland. Most arable farms are in the drier eastern areas, where the most fertile soil is to be found. In 1991 the agricultural labour force on main holdings numbered about 61,000, including full-time, part-time and casual workers as well as self-employed farmers. The value of gross agricultural output was £1,546 million.

The arable farms are highly productive, the principal crop being barley, which is used in the making of whisky and beer. Scotland's cattle industry has a worldwide reputation, both for the quality of meat and for pedigree breeds, such as Aberdeen Angus, Galloway and Highland. There are substantial sales of beef, mutton and lamb to England and exports to other countries in the European Community. The average dairy herd of about 90 cows, with Friesians predominating, is the largest among European Community countries. Production of poultrymeat has been expanding for a number of years. There is a limited area suitable for horticultural production, but the raspberry growing area in the Tayside region is among the largest in the world.

Loch Lomond—one of the most scenic areas in Britain.

The Edinburgh International Festival is one of the world's leading cultural events.

A production platform in BP's Magnus oilfield, north east of the Shetland Islands.

The Royal Bank of Scotland, Edinburgh. The Bank was founded in 1727 and operates throughout Britain.

The Glenfiddich whisky distillery at Dufftown, Grampian.

Over 13 million passenger journeys were made on the Glasgow Underground in 1991–92.

TRANSPORT AND COMMUNICATIONS

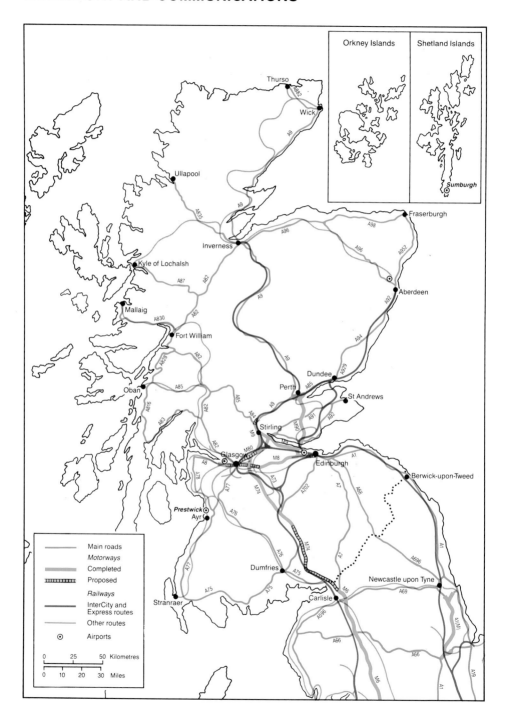

MAJOR CONSERVATION AND RECREATION AREAS

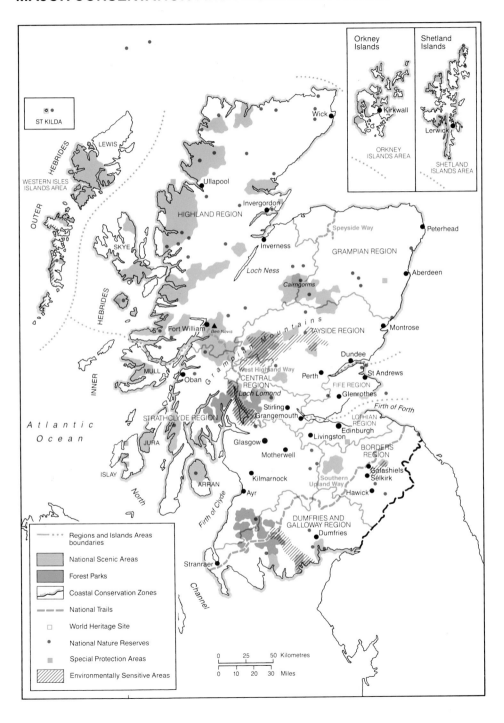

Orkney Islands

Shetland Islands

Kirkwall

ST KILDA

Wick

Lerwick

ORKNEY
ISLANDS AREA

SHETLAND
ISLANDS AREA

LEWIS

HEBRIDES

WESTERN ISLES
ISLANDS AREA

Ullapool

HIGHLAND REGION

OUTER

Invergordon

Speyside Way

Peterhead

SKYE

Inverness

GRAMPIAN REGION

Loch Ness

Aberdeen

HEBRIDES

Cairngorms

Montrose

Fort William

Ben Nevis

Grampian Mountains

TAYSIDE REGION

Dundee

West Highland Way

Perth

St Andrews

INNER

MULL

Oban

CENTRAL
REGION

FIFE REGION

Glenrothes

Loch Lomond

Stirling

Firth of Forth

STRATHCLYDE REGION

Grangemouth

LOTHIAN
REGION

*Atlantic
Ocean*

JURA

Glasgow

Livingston

Edinburgh

BORDERS
REGION

Motherwell

ISLAY

Galashiels
Selkirk

ARRAN

Kilmarnock

*Southern
Upland Way*

Ayr

Hawick

North

Firth of Clyde

DUMFRIES AND
GALLOWAY REGION

Dumfries

Stranraer

Channel

Legend

- - - - Regions and Islands Areas
boundaries

National Scenic Areas

Forest Parks

Coastal Conservation Zones

- - - National Trails

□ World Heritage Site

• National Nature Reserves

Special Protection Areas

Environmentally Sensitive Areas

0   25   50 Kilometres

0   10   20   30 Miles

A scientist at Edinburgh University uses the first commercially manufactured ion microprobe to be installed in a British university to learn more about the origins and evolution of the solar system.

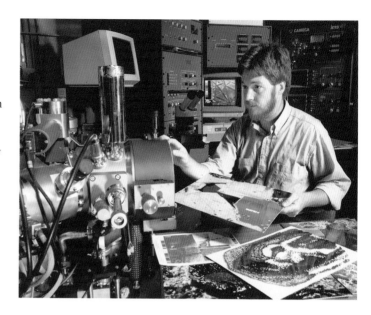

A remotely operated vehicle—developed by SubSea of Aberdeen—tackles a wellhead fire. The vehicle is designed to work in all kinds of hazardous environments.

A recreation ranger with a party of schoolchildren at species sighting posts in Aberfoyle, Central region.

The islands of St Kilda are one of 13 sites in Britain on the World Heritage List.

The Royal and Ancient golf course at St Andrews, whose Golf Club is the international governing body of the sport.

Tossing the caber at the Braemar Royal Highland Gathering.

Stephen Hendry—world snooker champion in 1990 and 1992.

Diversification

As an alternative to surplus production and to boost their income, farmers are being encouraged, through grants, to diversify into tourism and other non-agricultural activities on the farm. The Woodland Grant Scheme, together with the Farm Woodland Premium Scheme, offer grants and incentives to farmers to convert land in agricultural use to woodland. The European Community set-aside scheme, introduced in Britain in 1988, offers annual payments to farmers if they take at least 20 per cent of their arable land out of agricultural production for five years. An additional, temporary European Community set-aside scheme, introduced in Britain in 1991, offers a payment to farmers who take at least 15 per cent of their arable land, including 15 per cent of their cereals land, out of agricultural production for one year. Early in 1992 it was estimated that 2.6 per cent of arable land in Scotland (27,600 hectares out of nearly 1.1 million) had been set aside.

Crofting

Crofting agriculture, in the Highland region and the northern and western islands, is carried out by about 14,000 crofters (smallholders), who have traditionally supplemented their incomes from other forms of employment, such as fishing, knitting, weaving and, more recently, from tourism. The Crofters Commission is responsible for the regulation of crofting and administers a special system of grants. Crofters have security of tenure and since 1976 have been legally entitled to acquire ownership of their crofts. The Rural Enterprise Programme, launched in 1991, offers special funding, with Community support, to encourage farmers and crofters in designated areas in the Highlands and Islands to develop new business.

Environmentally Sensitive Areas

Five farming areas in Scotland which are of particular importance for their landscape, historic interest and wildlife have been designated as 'Environmentally Sensitive Areas' (ESAs). They are Loch Lomond (Strathclyde and Central regions), Breadalbane (mainly in Tayside), the Machair of the Uists and Benbecula (Western Isles), Whitlaw/Eildon (Borders) and Stewartry (Dumfries and Galloway). Farmers in ESAs are offered agreements under which they receive payments (partly funded by the European Community) for using farming methods which help to conserve the special character of the area.

The Government has announced plans to designate five new ESAs in Scotland. The new ESAs will be the Argyll Islands, the Shetland Islands, the Cairngorm Straths, the Western Southern Uplands, and the Central Southern Uplands. This new programme ensures that around 15 per cent of the total land area of Scotland will be included in an ESA, and represents £12 million of new expenditure.

Modern Practice and Research

The Royal Highland and Agricultural Society of Scotland, founded nearly two centuries ago, has been influential in spreading modern agricultural knowledge and practice, and its annual Royal Highland Show, held near Edinburgh, provides a showplace for the Scottish agricultural industry.

The Scottish Office Agriculture and Fisheries Department finances the national Scottish Agricultural College, which operates from three centres. The College carries out research and development work and provides an advisory service in addition to its educational function. The five Scottish Agricultural Research Institutes, funded by the Agriculture and Fisheries Department, include among their programmes work relevant to the soils, crops and livestock of northern Britain.

Forestry

Woodland covers about 15 per cent of Scotland, a higher proportion than in England, Wales or Northern Ireland. A main aim of government forestry policy is the steady expansion of tree cover to increase the diverse benefits that forests provide. Currently, there are some 1.05 million hectares (2.58 million acres) of forest in Scotland, of which about 516,000 hectares (1.27 million acres) are managed by the Forestry Commission's Forest Enterprise; the remainder is privately owned. The Commission is the government department responsible for forestry and the national forestry authority in Great Britain and has its headquarters in Edinburgh. The forestry industry in Scotland employs around 15,000 people. Total wood production is now some 2.3 million cubic metres a year. This is expected to double to nearly 5 million cubic metres by the early years of the twenty-first century as existing forests mature.

The Forestry Commission's expanded Woodland Grant Scheme provides grants for the creation of new woodlands and forests and the management and regeneration of existing ones. A special rate of grant is available to encourage the expansion of new native pine woods in the Highlands. A Central Scotland Woodland initiative aims to transform the landscape between Edinburgh and Glasgow by creating new and varied woodland with a wide range of environmental improvements.

Fishing

The fishing industry has traditionally been of major importance to Scotland and is still a significant source of employment, especially in the north east, the Islands and in some of the remoter coastal areas, where there are limited alternative employment opportunities. Scottish boats land about three-quarters by weight and over 60 per cent by value of all fish landed in Britain by British vessels. There are about 8,200 people employed on some 2,370 vessels. Many more people are employed in processing and other ancillary activities, such as boat building and net making. In 1991 the total value of the Scottish catch was £266.8 million, mainly comprising shellfish (£62.5 million), haddock (£49.9 million), cod (£43.2 million) and mackerel (£15.1 million). In terms of the value of landings, the principal ports are Peterhead (which has recently been enlarged) and Aberdeen.

Responsibility for fisheries protection rests with the Scottish Fisheries Protection Agency. This executive agency was created in 1991 within The Scottish Office Agriculture and Fisheries Department. It maintains a civilian fishery protection fleet and two civilian surveillance aircraft as well as using a Royal Navy vessel which operates mainly in the North Sea.

Fishing for salmon and sea trout is important to Scotland, both commercially and in relation to tourism. Another very popular activity is fishing for brown trout and other freshwater fish. Fish and shellfish farming continue to make a significant contribution to Scotland's rural infrastructure, especially in the Highlands and Islands. Scotland produces the largest amount of farmed salmon (40,600 tonnes in 1991) in the European Community.

In 1991 the fish and shellfish farming industries were estimated to have a combined wholesale turnover of some £130 million. Production is based on over 600 businesses operating from some 1,100 sites and employing about 2,000 people.

Government fisheries research and development is carried out by the Marine Laboratory at Aberdeen and the Freshwater Fisheries Laboratory at Pitlochry.

Transport and Communications

Roads

As in the rest of Britain, car ownership has increased, and in 1990, 58 per cent of households had the regular use of a car, 17 per cent having the use of two or more cars. At the end of 1990 there were nearly 1.8 million vehicles, including almost 1.6 million cars and light goods vehicles (311 per 1,000 population). There are nearly 52,000 km (32,000 miles) of publicly maintained roads in Scotland, of which over 3,200 km (2,000 miles) are trunk roads or motorways.

The three main motorways are the M8 Edinburgh-Glasgow-Greenock, the M9 Edinburgh-Stirling and the M90 Forth Road Bridge-Perth. These motorways, together with a good dual-carriageway system, provide a link between the main industrial areas in central and eastern Scotland. The A74 (Glasgow-Carlisle) is being upgraded to provide a dual three-lane northward extension of the M6 motorway, and the Central Scotland Motorway is to be completed. Another priority is the reconstruction of much of the A75 trunk road linking the Northern Ireland ferry ports of Stranraer and Cairnryan with the national motorway system. Further planned improvements to the strategic trunk road network throughout Scotland are set out in *Roads, Traffic and Safety*, published in March 1992 by The Scottish Office. It contains the Government's strategy for the rest of the 1990s, including a series of 'route action plans' designed to improve significantly safety and journey times on a number of major long-haul routes. The three main estuaries of central Scotland—those of the Clyde, Forth and

Tay—are spanned by road bridges, the last two of which are among the largest in Europe. Construction, improvement and maintenance of motorways and trunk roads are financed by the Government. Other roads are the responsibility of regional and islands councils.

Bus services were deregulated in 1986, and since then, bus and coach mileage has increased significantly. Local service provision increased from 285 million vehicle kilometres in 1985 to 338 million vehicle kilometres in 1989–90. In particular, there was a considerable increase in minibus services in towns and cities. The privatisation of the former Scottish Bus Group as ten separate companies is complete. The Strathclyde Passenger Transport Executive operates local bus services and an underground railway in Glasgow, and acts as the regional council's transport policy adviser throughout the Strathclyde area. In some of the less populated areas there are postbus services combining mail deliveries with facilities for passengers.

Rail

British Rail operates some 7,500 km (4,700 miles) of track and over 300 stations in Scotland. In 1990–91 there were some 55 million passenger journeys. The electrification of the main line between Edinburgh and London was completed in July 1991 at a cost of £450 million and provides services using InterCity 225 trains. An £80 million scheme to electrify services between Glasgow and Ayr, with a branch to Ardrossan, was completed in 1986. Commuter services operate between Glasgow, Edinburgh, Aberdeen and Dundee, and a Motorail network allows cars to be transported long distance by train. Freight services by rail are run on behalf of individual firms on scheduled timings, although freight traffic has declined considerably in recent years.

Ports and Waterways

Scottish ports provide direct container and conventional services to over 100 countries. East-coast ports trade chiefly with the rest of Europe, while west-coast trade is dominated by North America and other deep-sea trading areas. The most extensive port complexes are those on the Clyde and the Forth. The Clyde complex, Clydeport, combines the facilities of Glasgow and Greenock, the deep-water oil terminal at Finnart on Loch Long, and the coastal port of Ardrossan. On the Forth there are facilities at Grangemouth, Leith and Granton on the southern side of the Firth and at Burntisland, Kirkcaldy and Methil on the northern side. Cargo traffic on the Forth has increased—from 8.3 million tonnes in 1970 to 22.9 million tonnes in 1991—much of it related to off-shore oil and gas. The first purpose-built terminal for oil from the British sector of the North Sea was completed at Hound Point on the Forth in 1975. The port of Stranraer handles most of the traffic to and from Ireland.

Other major port developments undertaken to handle traffic generated by offshore oil and gas include the terminals at Flotta and Sullom Voe. Three of the four jetties at Sullom Voe can handle tankers of up to 350,000 deadweight tons, and the fourth jetty handles the export of liquified petroleum gases, accommodating vessels with a capacity of up to 75,000 cubic metres. A £54 million terminal at Braefoot Bay in the Firth of Forth handles tankers carrying natural gas liquids brought from the plant at Mossmorran in Fife. Supply bases for offshore vessels have been built at Leith, Dundee, Montrose, Aberdeen, Peterhead and Lerwick.

Passenger and freight services are operated to all the island groups, with roll-on/roll-off ferries on most routes. The most important operator is Caledonian MacBrayne, which is nationally owned. Services to Orkney and Shetland are provided by P & O Scottish Ferries.

The principal inland waterways open to navigation are the Caledonian Canal, from Fort William to Inverness, and the Crinan Canal through the Mull of Kintyre. Although both are used by fishing and commercial craft, their main use is by pleasure yachts.

Airports

With the improvement and extension of facilities at Scottish airports, passenger and freight traffic has grown rapidly. Services include direct intercontinental flights, flights to the rest of Britain and Europe, and local flights to and from the islands. Services are operated by a number of airlines, including British Airways, British Midland Airways and Loganair. The main airports are at Glasgow, Edinburgh, Prestwick and Aberdeen, of which all except Prestwick are owned and managed by Scottish Airports Ltd (a subsidiary of BAA plc). Sumburgh airport in Shetland and seven smaller airfields in the Highlands and Islands are controlled by a public body, Highlands and Islands Airports Ltd. A £35 million project to upgrade Scotland's air traffic control system was announced by the Government in January 1992.

In 1991 Scottish airports handled nearly 9.9 million passengers (including transit passengers), of whom 4.3 million passed through Glasgow, 2.4 million through Edinburgh, and just over 2 million through Aberdeen.

Telecommunications

The telecommunications services sector is one of the growth areas of the economy. Following the Telecommunications Act 1984, British Telecom's exclusive privilege of running public telecommunications systems was removed, and Mercury Communications Ltd (a subsidiary of Cable and Wireless plc) was licensed as the second national fixed-link operator. Edinburgh and Glasgow are connected by optical fibre to Mercury Communications' national trunk telecommunications network, and in Edinburgh a local optical fibre network has been installed to enable residents to benefit from direct connection to the national trunk cable.

Environment

Planning

There are two levels of land use planning.[7] Structure plans ident-
ify broad strategic objectives and are the responsibility of regional
and islands councils. They must be formally approved by the
Secretary of State for Scotland. Local plans deal with detailed planning on a local basis and are, with some exceptions, looked after by
district councils. Provided they do not conflict with the objectives
of the regional structure plan or involve issues of national importance, they may be implemented without reference to the Secretary
of State.

An application for planning permission must be made for
most kinds of development, other than minor changes such as small
alterations to dwelling houses. In enterprise zones and simplified
planning zones advance planning permission is given for specified
types of development. There is provision for appeals against deci-
sions of the planning authority and for public inquiries by a small
staff of inquiry reporters, who are part of The Scottish Office.

Housing

Scotland's housing stock in 1990 amounted to 2,124,000 dwellings,
over 121,000 more than the number of households. Since 1981 the
rate of private house-building has been increasing, while in the
public sector the emphasis has shifted from new building to

[7]For more information on planning see *Planning* (Aspects of Britain series).

modernisation and improvement, and particularly to the regeneration of large housing estates in urban areas.

Home ownership is increasing but, at 53 per cent, is still lower than in other areas of Britain, while the proportion of public sector dwellings, rented from local authorities, Scottish Homes and new towns, has decreased to 38 per cent. Under the Housing (Scotland) Act 1987, most public sector tenants have security of tenure and are entitled, subject to the satisfaction of certain basic qualifying conditions, to buy their homes on favourable terms. Nearly 178,000 local authority houses have been sold to sitting tenants since the introduction of an earlier Act in 1980.

Housing associations in Scotland are supported by Scottish Homes, a housing development agency set up in 1989 under the Housing (Scotland) Act 1988. Scottish Homes incorporated the Housing Corporation in Scotland and the Scottish Special Housing Association. It provides financial assistance to housing associations, and owns and manages housing in its own right. Its 1992–93 expenditure programme is expected to be about £333 million, of which about £220 million is going to housing associations. Scottish Homes pioneered a 'Rents to Mortgages' scheme, which in April 1991 was extended to local authority tenants.

Repair and improvement grants are available for works to houses in private ownership including houses which fall below the tolerable standard or lack all of the standard amenities.

Urban Renewal

The Government is continuing to tackle urban deprivation in Scotland. In 1988 it set out in the White Paper *New Life for Urban Scotland* its strategy for improving conditions on peripheral estates. Building on the experience gained from inner city regeneration schemes, the main aim is to encourage residents to take more responsibility for the revitalisation of their communities.

The focus of this effort was the establishment of four partnerships led by The Scottish Office and involving other bodies and groups, including Scottish Enterprise, Scottish Homes, the local authorities, the private sector and the local communities. The four partnerships have been set up in areas of Dundee, Edinburgh, Glasgow and Paisley. Expenditure by central government and its agencies is expected to be some £40 million in 1992–93. The partnerships' objectives include plans to:

—improve the housing available to local people;

—improve employment prospects by facilitating access to training and further education; and

—tackle social and environmental problems on the estates.

Other peripheral estates and inner city areas continue to receive substantial assistance through such sources as the Urban Programme. Through this Programme, the Government has provided grants of 75 per cent towards the cost of over 1,200 projects tackling deprivation in urban areas. The Urban Programme in Scotland has grown from £44 million in 1988–89 to over £81 million in 1992–93.

Scottish Enterprise also works to encourage private sector investment for projects in deprived areas through a number of funding arrangements.

Conservation and Wildlife

The natural beauty of Scotland's rugged and mountainous landscape is enjoyed in increasing numbers by local people and tourists, and conservation has become a matter of considerable public concern, as elsewhere in Britain. Statutory and voluntary organisations co-operate to protect the countryside from inappropriate development, to preserve historic buildings and monuments and to safeguard wildlife and natural habitats.

A new organisation, Scottish Natural Heritage (SNH), was set up in April 1992, with responsibility for nature and landscape conservation and countryside recreation. It has taken over the functions carried out in Scotland by the former Nature Conservancy Council and the Countryside Commission for Scotland. SNH gives advice to the Government and to all those whose activities affect wildlife and the countryside. Planned expenditure in 1992–93 totals nearly £35 million.

There are 68 national nature reserves in Scotland and 1,340 Sites of Special Scientific Interest. Four regional parks and 40 'national scenic areas' have been designated, covering a total of 13 per cent of the country's land surface. These are subject to special planning arrangements under which certain kinds of development are subject to consultation with SNH and, in the event of a disagreement, with the Secretary of State. Five farming areas have been designated as Environmentally Sensitive Areas (see p. 50), and conservation of the environment is also a high priority of the Forestry Commission (see p. 51). Four of the 11 forest parks in Great Britain are in Scotland, and a fifth spans the border between Scotland and England. There are also 36 country parks.

The Natural Heritage (Scotland) Act 1991 provides for the designation of Natural Heritage Areas (NHAs) by the Secretary for State. Once designated, an NHA will create a general framework within which the outstanding natural heritage importance of an area can be recognised by sensitive and sustainable management. The Government has asked SNH to prepare recommendations for implementing this designation in areas where it would provide a clear benefit to natural heritage management.

The Cairngorms Working Party submitted a strategy report to the Government in autumn 1992. Following government consideration of the report, a case for listing the Cairngorms as a World Heritage Site of natural importance will be prepared.[8] A working party is also considering a management strategy for Loch Lomond and the Trossachs.

Scotland's countryside contains a rich variety of wildlife, with some species unknown elsewhere in Britain. Wild animals found in Scotland include the pine marten, wild cat, mountain hare, red squirrel, roe deer and red deer. Bird species include the ptarmigan, golden eagle, osprey, capercaillie (wood-grouse), red grouse and black grouse. Nature reserves, bird sanctuaries and other designated areas provide opportunities for the protection and study of some of the rarer fauna and flora.

Local authorities and a variety of amenity organisations are concerned with the conservation of historic buildings. Under the provisions of planning law, buildings of special architectural or historic interest are listed and may not be demolished or altered without consent from the local authority. There are some 38,000 listed buildings and over 5,500 scheduled monuments in Scotland. There is also provision for the designation by local authorities of 'conservation areas' of special character. Grants are available for the repair and restoration of historic buildings and for the enhancement of listed buildings and conservation areas. Central government grants are made on the advice of Historic Scotland—an executive agency of The Scottish Office—which manages some 330 monuments in its care.

[8]The islands of St Kilda are one of 13 sites in Britain on the World Heritage List. For further information see *Conservation* (Aspects of Britain series).

Among voluntary organisations concerned with conservation, the National Trust for Scotland, founded in 1931, has the statutory duty of promoting the care of fine buildings, historic places and beautiful countryside. It owns or cares for some of the most outstanding scenery and buildings in the country, with more than 100 properties, including castles and other historic buildings and some 40,000 hectares (over 100,000 acres). It has some 234,500 members, and in 1991 over 2 million people visited its properties. The Trust negotiates conservation agreements with landlords and has made special efforts to protect unspoiled coastline, particularly in areas under pressure from oil-related or similar development.

Other bodies concerned with conservation, wildlife and environmental issues in Scotland include the Scottish Civic Trust, the Association for the Protection of Rural Scotland, the Royal Commission on Ancient and Historical Monuments of Scotland, the Saltire Society (which, among other activities, makes awards for the restoration of buildings of special architectural merit), the Scottish Wildlife Trust and the Royal Society for the Protection of Birds.

Control of Pollution

Executive responsibility for pollution control is divided between local authorities and central government agencies. The Secretary of State for Scotland is responsible for pollution control co-ordination. River purification authorities have statutory responsibility for water pollution control. Earlier in 1992 the Government consulted on its proposal to create a new Scottish Environment Protection Agency.

Under the Environmental Protection Act 1990, a system of 'integrated pollution control' (IPC) was introduced in April 1992 to control certain categories of industrial pollution. IPC is administered jointly by Her Majesty's Industrial Pollution Inspectorate and the river purification authorities.

The Water Quality Survey of Scotland in 1990 found that the proportion of unpolluted rivers, lochs and canals had risen from 95.3 per cent in 1985 to 97 per cent.

Social Welfare

Health Services

In 1948 a comprehensive National Health Service (NHS) was introduced in Scotland, similar to the service adopted for the rest of Britain, but with some differences in the details of administration. Central responsibility lies with the Secretary of State for Scotland, who acts through The Scottish Office Home and Health Department. Gross expenditure on the NHS is planned to grow from £3,433 million in 1991–92 to £3,725 million in 1992–93, rising to £4,030 million in 1994–95.

Responsibility for the provision of most of the services is delegated to 15 Health Boards, each in charge of an area. The Boards co-operate closely with local authorities, which are responsible for social work and environmental and other services. In recent years priority has been given to preventive medicine and to caring for people in the community rather than in institutions, and there have been substantial increases in primary health care staff.

The National Health Service and Community Care Act 1990 has introduced wide-ranging changes in management and patient care in the health and social care services. These changes, which came into effect in 1991, aim to give patients, wherever they live in Britain, better health care and greater choice of services. The NHS continues to be open to all, regardless of their income, and there has been greater delegation of decision-making and financial responsibility to hospitals and general practices at local level.

Health authority expenditure is financed mainly from general taxation. Most medical treatment under the NHS is free to patients, although there are set charges for dental and ophthalmic services (with exemptions for certain categories of patient, such as children and expectant mothers).

General medical, dental and ophthalmic services outside the hospitals are provided by independent practitioners. The major teaching hospitals in the cities provide specialised treatment for surrounding areas. A Common Services Agency handles those services which are most efficiently organised centrally for the whole of Scotland, including ambulance and blood transfusion services.

Most cases of illness are dealt with solely by general practitioners (GPs), who are mainly in the NHS and under contract to provide a full range of primary medical care. On average, each GP has about 1,600 patients on his or her list. In the sparsely populated Highlands and Islands, arrangements are made to ensure that everyone has a family doctor available reasonably close at hand. There were some 3,380 doctors in practice in 1991. Many doctors work in partnerships or group practices, often as members of a health care team which may also include health visitors, district nurses, midwives and social workers. The team may be based in a health centre, which provides purpose-built and well-equipped surgeries for a range of health services.

A nationwide breast cancer screening service has been set up for all women between 50 and 64, who should all have their mammography screening invitations by 1994. All Health Boards have also been asked to establish a fully computerised call and recall system for cervical cancer screening and to ensure that all women between 20 and 60 are invited to attend by the end of 1993.

Treatment for people with mental handicaps or mental illness is increasingly taking the form of care in the community and the provision of day hospital facilities. This pattern of care is also being developed for the medical care of elderly people.

Hospitals

There are over 300 hospitals in the Scottish health service, with a total of about 50,640 available beds and employing some 11,000 doctors. The number of patients treated continues to grow; in 1991–92 nearly 918,500 in-patients were treated. Hospital buildings range from small cottage hospitals in the rural areas to major teaching complexes linked with universities. Since 1979, 87 major health building projects have been completed, providing approximately 8,500 beds, and a further 43 schemes are under development. Scotland's first heart transplant unit opened in Glasgow in 1991. Two hospitals became self-governing NHS trust hospitals—independent of Health Board control—in April 1992 and others are considering the possibility of adopting trust status.

Scotland has a long-established reputation in the field of medical education and research, and about 600 doctors graduate annually from Scottish medical schools. The Scottish Hospital Advisory Service provides information and advice on the management of mental and geriatric hospitals.

The Scottish Ambulance Service includes an Air Ambulance Service to carry patients from the Western Isles, Orkney and Shetland and from the more remote parts of the mainland to the larger hospital centres.

Health Education and Improvement

Health education is the responsibility of the Health Education Board for Scotland, which provides training and materials on health education. The Board also runs publicity campaigns designed to inform the public about good health practice and dangers such as coronary heart disease, smoking, alcohol and drug misuse and AIDS. Government provision for the Health Education Board in 1992–93 is £6.5 million, a 25 per cent increase on the previous year.

Key indicators of health show continuing improvement in Scotland. Between 1983 and 1990 life expectancy at birth increased from 69.6 to 71.1 years for men and from 75.7 years to 76.9 years for women. Over the same period infant mortality decreased from 9.9 per thousand births to 7.7.

Despite improvements, however, Scotland's health record compares unfavourably with that of other Western industrialised countries. In particular, death rates are persistently higher for the major causes of death such as cancer, heart attacks and strokes. Against this background, priorities and targets for health improvements in the major areas have been set by the Government. Most recently these were set out in July 1992 in the policy document *Scotland's Health: A Challenge to Us All* (see Further Reading). Major initiatives identified to support the efforts already in progress include:

—moves to encourage a change in dietary habits, with experimental projects being undertaken in selected Urban Partnership areas to encourage the adoption of healthy diets;

—a specialist group appointed by the Chief Medical Officer to develop national dietary targets and advice;

—a new target of reducing coronary heart disease by 40 per cent between 1990 and 2000 for those aged under 65;

—the commissioning of a Scottish Health Survey to assess the state of health of the population;

—the development of a national dental strategy;

—additional funding for the Health Education Board for Scotland; and

—the establishment of a resource centre for health education.

Social Work Services

An important area of local authority responsibility in Scotland is that of social welfare. In recent years there has been an increasing demand for services for the most vulnerable members of the community, including elderly people, children in need of care, and people with mental illness or with physical or mental handicap. Each local authority's social work services are organised under a single social work department, so that individuals, families or groups with a number of separate needs or problems may turn to a single source for help and guidance.

The Secretary of State for Scotland has general responsibility for the oversight of the social work services provided by local authorities and independent bodies and is assisted by the Social Work Services Group of The Scottish Office Home and Health Department. The Group undertakes a range of duties in connection with research and training, financial assistance to voluntary organisations and certain other matters. Social work training in Scotland is accredited by the Central Council for Education and Training in Social Work, a British body, and courses are provided to degree level and beyond.

Local authority social workers have close links with the National Health Service, and some 500 work in hospital social work units. They also work closely with the police, with the housing, planning and education departments of local authorities, and with the many statutory and voluntary bodies. Services offered increasingly reflect the emphasis on caring in the community rather than institutional provision, and are wide ranging. They include child care and supervision; care of elderly people and those with a physical handicap; facilities for mentally ill and mentally disabled people; administering community service by offenders; supervising probation and the after-care of prisoners; and attending to the social welfare of the community.

The recent reforms in community care provision, which take effect between April 1991 and April 1993, establish a new financial and managerial framework. They are intended to enable vulnerable groups in the community to live as normal a life as possible in their own homes, and to give them a greater say in how they live and how the services that they need should be provided. Local authorities and Health Boards have drawn up community care plans after consultation with the voluntary sector and other interested parties.

Child Care

Closely linked with local authority social work departments is the system of children's hearings (see p. 22). All children up to the age of 16 who are in need of compulsory care (other than those who have committed very serious offences) fall within the scope of the hearings system, and most are allowed to remain at home under the supervision of a social worker. There are a number of intensive group work programmes, where children in trouble may be helped within their own environment and without the need for residential care. For certain children considered by a children's hearing to require compulsory residential care there are about 18 schools mainly run by voluntary bodies. Children taken into care for other reasons are accommodated in some 150 residential homes, most of which are managed by local authorities.

A review of child care legislation in Scotland has been carried out and its results are under consideration.

Elderly and Disabled People

Local authorities and voluntary bodies continue to develop their services for elderly people living in their own homes, including the provision of home helps and 'meals on wheels' (hot midday meals brought by van). Residential care is available in 281 local authority and 359 registered voluntary homes, with a total of about 18,000 places. There are day-care centres and recreational, social and lunch clubs for the elderly.

Services, other than medical, for physically and mentally disabled people include residential homes and day-care centres run by local authorities or voluntary organisations. Local authorities also undertake the adaptation of houses to make them suitable for occupation by disabled people. Typical alterations include the installation of ground-floor toilets or ramps for wheelchairs.

Education

Although educational policy is broadly similar throughout Britain, the Scottish system has retained a number of distinctive features and practices. Public education is administered centrally by The Scottish Office Education Department and locally by the nine regional and three islands education authorities, which are responsible for school and most post-school education in their areas. However, responsibility for further education will be transferred to the Secretary of State for Scotland in April 1993. University education is the responsibility of the Department for Education in London.

The Secretary of State for Scotland has general oversight of the work of education authorities, including their school building programmes. Central institutions and colleges of education (see p. 77) are managed by independent governing bodies whose members represent appropriate interests in education, the professions, industry, commerce and the arts. Education is financed by government grants and local taxes.

Schools

As in the rest of Britain, compulsory schooling begins at the age of 5 and ends at the age of 16. Nearly all schools are administered by the education authorities and maintained by public funds, and are known as public schools. Most of the education authority schools are comprehensive, co-educational and non-denominational, and all must conform with standards prescribed in regulations made by the Secretary of State. There are about 2,800 education authority primary and secondary schools, with about 735,000 pupils.

Parents have a statutory right to express a preference for a particular school for their children. Moreover, the Government has decided that more information should be made available to parents about their child's school and other schools. The information would cover examination results, attendancy and truancy rates, school leaver destinations, and school costs.

Education authorities are required to establish School Boards, consisting of elected parent and staff members as well as co-opted members. The Boards play a significant part in public school administration and management. Parents of children at public schools where there is a School Board can opt for local self-management following a ballot. If they vote in favour and the Secretary of State accepts the School Board's application for self-governing status, the school is funded directly by The Scottish Office Education Department.

There are 200 fee-charging private independent schools with 34,600 pupils. An Assisted Places Scheme provides remission of fees for children whose parents prefer private education but who are unable to afford the full costs of the fees charged.

In Gaelic-speaking areas education authorities are required to make adequate provision for the teaching of Gaelic. Religious education must be included in the curriculum, but content is determined by education authorities and schools in accordance with the wishes of the local community. Parents are entitled to withdraw their children from such classes and there are safeguards for individual conscience.

For children under 5 there are nursery schools and classes, play groups and day nurseries. Primary schools take children between the ages of 5 and 12, normally providing infant classes for children under the age of 7.

There is a range of specialist provision for children with special educational needs, although it is policy that, wherever possible, such children should attend mainstream schools.

Curriculum

A major review of the curriculum for the 5- to 14-year age range has resulted in new guidelines being issued by the Government on all aspects of the curriculum and on assessment of pupils' progress. Standardised tests in English and mathematics have been introduced for these school years. Guidance on both primary and secondary curricula is issued by The Scottish Office Education Department and the Scottish Consultative Council on the Curriculum.

Up to the fourth year of secondary education the general aim is to provide a well-balanced curriculum for all pupils, and all children up to the age of 16 have to study English, mathematics and science. The Consultative Council has recommended that secondary school pupils should follow a broad and balanced curriculum consisting of English, mathematics, science, a modern European language, social studies, technological activities, art, music or drama, religious and moral education and physical education. It is the Government's view that pupils should normally study a modern foreign language during the four compulsory years of secondary school.

Examinations

The main school examination is the Scottish Certificate of Education (SCE). The SCE standard grade caters for the whole ability range and is taken at the end of the fourth year of secondary education. Grades are awarded on a single seven-point scale, which is divided into three levels of performance; pupils are assessed against criteria for each of the three levels. All pupils receive a certificate which shows the grades achieved and a grade for overall performance.

Pupils in the fifth and sixth years of secondary education sit the SCE Higher grade. Passes at this grade are required for entry to degree courses at colleges and universities or for entry to professional training. The Certificate of Sixth Year Studies is intended for those who have completed Higher grade studies and who wish to continue studies in particular subjects; work is similar to that in the initial stages of degree courses. The Scottish Examination Board runs SCE examinations and awards certificates. Some 77 per cent of 16-year-olds stay on at school or enter further education, representing a proportion significantly greater than the average for Britain.

A review of courses and examinations for those aged 16 to 18 was instituted in 1990. The committee's report was issued early in 1992 and is being considered by the Government.

Technical and Vocational Education
The Technical and Vocational Education Initiative, a national programme for those aged 14 to 18, was introduced in 1984. It promotes technical and vocational education in the context of a broader curriculum. There is also a system of vocational education for 16- to 18-year-olds based on short units of study or 'modules' of varying degrees of difficulty. These cover a wide range of theoretical and practical work. Modules are available to school pupils or through part-time attendance at a further education college and are certificated by the Scottish Vocational Education Council (SCOTVEC).

Teachers and Teacher Training

All teachers in education authority schools must be registered with the General Teaching Council for Scotland, a statutory body which acts as the Secretary of State's main adviser on the training and supply of teachers. Pre-service teacher training courses for both primary and secondary sectors are conducted at five teacher training institutions financed by the Scottish Office Education Department and administered by independent governing bodies. The University of Stirling offers courses combining academic and professional training for prospective teachers.

The Government's policy since 1987 has been that all entrants to the Scottish teaching profession should be graduates. New primary school teachers qualify either through a four-year Bachelor of Education (B.Ed) course or a one-year postgraduate course of teacher education. Secondary school teachers must have a degree containing two passes in the subjects that they wish to teach and must also have undertaken a one-year postgraduate course. For teachers of music or technology, four-year B.Ed courses are also available. Teachers of physical education take a B.Ed course at Moray House Institute of Education in Edinburgh.

In 1991–92 there were 46,500 teachers in education authority schools, with a pupil-teacher ratio of 19.5:1 in primary schools and 12.2:1 in secondary schools. These are significantly lower than ratios in many other parts of Britain.

Post-school Education

Post-school education is provided on a full-time and part-time basis at 45 further education colleges presently managed by education authorities; 14 higher education institutions; independently managed colleges, including five colleges of education offering advanced education in a range of vocationally oriented subjects; and 12 universities.

The higher education institutions and some of the further education colleges provide most of the advanced-level (post Higher grade) courses leading to Higher National Certificates (HNCs) or Higher National Diplomas (HNDs), to degrees or other professional or technical qualifications recognised as the equivalent of degrees. Subjects taught include science, technology, art, architecture, business and management studies, social studies, music, drama, home economics, textiles and agriculture. Higher education institutions and further education colleges have links with commerce, industry and the professions. Most funding for further education colleges is currently provided by education authorities, but will be provided by The Scottish Office Education Department from April 1993. From then all higher education institutions which are designated by the Secretary of State will be funded, along with the universities, by the Scottish Higher Education Funding Council. The Privy Council may confer degree-awarding powers on any designated institution which meets the criteria. Dundee Institute of Technology also offers research degrees.

Courses at the further education colleges are provided on a full- or part-time basis and in general at sub-degree level. They provide training at non-advanced level for operatives, craftsmen and at advanced level (HNC/HND) for technicians and their equivalents in agriculture, industry and commerce. The Scottish Vocational Education Council is responsible for accrediting vocational qualifications in Scotland and also prepares and awards most such qualifications. The management of 43 of the further education colleges will be transferred from local education authorities to new college boards of management in April 1993. Colleges will become self-governing and receive finance directly from central government.

The Professional, Industrial and Commercial Updating Programme (PICKUP) is designed to help institutions of further and higher education update and broaden the skills of those in mid-career in industry, commerce and the professions. The Scottish Wider Access Programme is aimed at able students who do not have the traditional entry qualifications to gain access to higher education.

Education for adults is provided by the education authorities, largely through further education colleges and sometimes in co-operation with university extramural departments, higher educa-tion institutions and voluntary bodies. Courses and classes are offered in vocational and academic subjects at all levels and also in cultural and recreational subjects. Under 'Open Learning' pro-grammes, users study at home or in the workplace, with audio and video tapes and computer-based equipment, backed up by advice and help from training centres. Work-based learning is also avail-able. The Open College extends access to vocational education and training by broadcasting open-learning courses on television and radio throughout Britain.

The Scottish Community Education Council advises the Government on community and adult education, including adult literacy and basic education, to enable adults to cope with the demands of a modern industrialised society.

Universities

Scotland has 12 universities. St Andrews, Glasgow and Aberdeen were founded in the fifteenth century and Edinburgh in the sixteenth. Four others—Strathclyde, Heriot-Watt, Dundee and Stirling—were established in the 1960s. Strathclyde and Heriot-Watt developed from former central institutions and Dundee from a constituent college of St Andrews University. Stirling was an entirely new foundation. The remaining four gained university status under the provisions of the Further and Higher Education (Scotland) Act 1992: Napier University (in Edinburgh), the Robert Gordon University (in Aberdeen), the Glasgow Caledonian University (to be formed by the merger of Glasgow Polytechnic and the Queens College, Glasgow) and the University of Paisley. Glasgow Polytechnic, the fourth, meets all the criteria for university status and its name remains to be decided.

Most of the universities' income is drawn from a block grant made by the Government and distributed to the universities on the advice of the Universities Funding Council. The Council has a Scottish Committee, which considers issues affecting all aspects of higher education in Scotland. From April 1993 the Council and Committee will be superseded by the Scottish Higher Education Funding Council (see p. 78).

In 1990–91 some 97,000 students were in full-time higher education in Scotland. There were also nearly 8,000 students taking courses with the Open University, which provides degree and other courses on a part-time basis, making use of television, radio, correspondence courses and summer schools.

Despite many changes, the Scottish universities have retained their traditional emphasis on breadth of study. The three-year ordinary degree course in arts or science (BA or BSc), requiring passes in a range of subjects, continues to be the choice of a high proportion of students. An additional year's study is required for an honours degree in arts or science, while other subjects, such as medicine and theology, require five or six years' study. All universities offer higher degrees and facilities for research. A number of mergers involving universities and higher education institutions have been proposed—the final decision will rest with the Secretary of State.

Youth and Community Services

There is close co-operation between education authorities and voluntary organisations in the encouragement of youth and community services and the provision of centres, clubs, camps and recreation grounds. Although most groups and organisations are run by voluntary bodies, grants are available from public funds towards the salaries of organisers and for leadership training. In many areas, education authorities provide accommodation for youth and community activities, often in school premises. The Scottish Community Education Council supports individuals and organisations working in this field, and The Scottish Office Education Department gives grants to voluntary organisations. Full-time professional training courses are offered at some of the colleges of education.

Culture

Promotion of the Arts

Innovation and experiment in drama, art and music have led in recent years to a vigorous cultural and artistic scene, which is strongly supported by local authorities, private trusts and commercial concerns. One of the principal modern contributions to the arts has been the Edinburgh International Festival of Music and Drama, inaugurated in 1947. Held annually in August, it is the largest of its kind in the world and has provided a focus and inspiration for creative activity in the arts. Other annual festivals in Edinburgh include international folk and jazz festivals and the Film and Television Festival.

Glasgow too has developed into an important artistic centre. For 1990 Glasgow was designated by the European Community as the European City of Culture, and provided an extensive programme of cultural events. These included the commissioning of 30 major new works in the performing and visual arts; 40 world premieres in theatre, dance and music; 125 exhibitions; 1,200 performances and 60 sporting events. Visits by tourists to arts events in Glasgow in 1990 rose by 81 per cent compared with 1986, and attendance at theatres, galleries, halls and museums increased by 40 per cent. The year produced an estimated net return to the regional economy of between £10 million and £14 million. In addition, Glasgow has held since 1982 its own international arts festival, the Mayfest, which is now the second largest festival in Britain.

Other cities and towns run their own festivals, and amateur arts festivals are held throughout the country, including the

National Gaelic Mod, an annual celebration of the music, poetry and song of the Gael, organised by An Comunn Gaidhealach (the Highland Association).

The Arts Council of Great Britain, represented in Scotland by the Scottish Arts Council, is the main agency for distributing government funds in support of the arts, operating through committees dealing respectively with art, drama, literature and music. Its activities include sponsoring tours in Scotland by both Scottish and non-Scottish artists and co-operating with regional and local bodies concerned with the arts. It also encourages Scotland's own cultural traditions and fosters work in schools and among young people.

National organisations with an interest in the arts include the Royal Society of Edinburgh, founded in 1783 for the promotion of science and literature; the Royal Fine Art Commission for Scotland; the Saltire Society, formed to conserve and foster the Scottish way of life through architecture and the arts; and An Comunn Gaidhealach, which promotes the Gaelic language and culture. The conservation work of the National Trust for Scotland (see p. 64) preserves valuable elements of Scotland's cultural past.

Music, Drama and Ballet

Highlights of Scotland's contemporary artistic development have included the formation of Scottish Opera and Scottish Ballet. Scottish Opera, based in Glasgow, has gained an international reputation since its foundation in 1962, while Scottish Ballet, also based in Glasgow, has a repertoire of classical and contemporary works; both companies take programmes to schools. The Royal Scottish Orchestra and the Scottish Chamber Orchestra make regular tours in Scotland as well as visits to England and overseas, and are prominent in promoting modern music. Another important professional orchestra is the BBC Scottish Symphony Orchestra, which broadcasts extensively on both BBC Radio Scotland and BBC Radio 3. It also performs throughout Scotland and tours regularly in Europe. In 1990 a new international concert hall was opened in Glasgow. The hall is the new home of the Scottish National Orchestra and has a 2,500-seat auditorium, making it the largest of its kind in Britain.

Regional theatres have been established in Glasgow, Edinburgh, Dundee, Aberdeen and Perth. The Pitlochry Festival Theatre gives an annual summer season in a setting of great scenic beauty, drawing audiences from a wide area. The Traverse Theatre in Edinburgh, with a theatre workshop attached, undertakes experimental work, while the Glasgow Citizens' Theatre has an international reputation as one of the most adventurous theatre companies in Britain. There are many small theatres and touring groups throughout the country. The Scottish Youth Theatre in Glasgow offers early acting opportunities to young people.

Amateur interest in the arts is maintained by many local groups, helped and encouraged by a wide range of voluntary organisations. Traditional Highland dancing and piping are widely practised by both amateurs and professionals. Professional training in music and dramatic art is centred at the Royal Scottish Academy of Music and Drama in Glasgow.

Museums and Galleries

Scotland's national collections are held by the National Museums of Scotland and the National Galleries of Scotland. The National Museums of Scotland include the Royal Museum of Scotland and the Scottish United Services Museum, both in Edinburgh; the Museum of Flight, near North Berwick; the Scottish Agricultural Museum, at Ingliston; and the Shambellie House Museum of Costume, near Dumfries. A new Museum of Scotland is to be built next to the Royal Museum to house the National Museums' Scottish collection. The National Galleries of Scotland comprise the National Gallery of Scotland, the Scottish National Portrait Gallery and the Scottish National Gallery of Modern Art. Government provision for the National Museums of Scotland and National Galleries of Scotland in 1992–93 is about £23 million. In 1991 the National Museums received over 1 million visitors and the National Galleries about 700,000.

There are important municipal art collections in Edinburgh, Glasgow, Perth, Dundee and Aberdeen, and many smaller towns such as Inverness, Stirling, Kirkcaldy and Kingussie have interesting museums and galleries. In Glasgow the world-famous Burrell Collection of tapestries, paintings and *objets d'art* opened in 1983 in a new £20.5 million museum. The Royal Scottish Academy in Edinburgh mounts an annual exhibition of works by contemporary artists, and the Scottish Arts Council has a travelling gallery and gives financial aid to private galleries, art centres and individual artists. In 1992–93 the Government will provide £675,000, through the Scottish Museum Council, for local museums. The Scottish Design Centre in Glasgow encourages high standards of quality and design.

Literature and Libraries

Funds allocated to literature by the Scottish Arts Council are used to encourage creative writing through awards to authors and publishers, the establishment of creative writing fellowships at universities, and grants to literary magazines. The study of literature is included in the curricula of all schools and universities and, as throughout Britain, local authorities operate a free public library system (whose origin owes much to the Scottish-born benefactor Andrew Carnegie, 1835–1918). In 1991 there were nearly 700 public libraries run by Scottish local authorities. The National Library of Scotland, established in Edinburgh in 1682, is a copyright library entitled to receive a copy of every new book published in Britain. Its collections include early and rare Scottish books and pamphlets. A new building to house the Scottish Science Library was opened in 1989. Among other important libraries are the Mitchell Library in Glasgow, the Signet Library in Edinburgh, and the Library of the Royal Society of Edinburgh. All the universities have considerable library resources, some containing collections specifically related to Scotland.

Scotland continues to be an important book-publishing centre, especially of literary, educational and theological works. The Gaelic Book Council, funded by the Scottish Arts Council, provides assistance for the publication of books in Scottish Gaelic.

Films

The promotion of film is undertaken by the Scottish Film Council. It supports a number of regional film theatres, administers the Scottish Film Archive, and promotes and provides material for media education. Together with the Scottish Arts Council, it has set up the Scottish Film Production Fund, which makes grants towards film and video production in Scotland. It gives financial assistance to projects which contribute to the growth of a national cinema reflecting contemporary Scottish society and culture.

Press and Broadcasting

Scotland's strong journalistic tradition dates back to 1699, when the *Edinburgh Gazette* first appeared. In relation to its population Scotland produces a large number of newspapers and periodicals. Six morning, six evening and four Sunday newspapers are published, as well as over 100 weekly and local newspapers. Of the morning papers, the *Herald* (formerly the *Glasgow Herald*), first published in 1783, and *The Scotsman*, founded in 1817 and published in Edinburgh, take an independent editorial line and have a considerable circulation outside Scotland. Other morning papers are the *Aberdeen Press and Journal* (first published as the *Aberdeen Journal* in 1748); the *Dundee Courier and Advertiser*; the *Daily Record*, a popular newspaper published in Glasgow; and the *Scottish Daily Express*. Evening papers are published in Aberdeen, Dundee, Edinburgh, Glasgow, Greenock and Paisley. The Sunday publications comprise the *Sunday Mail*, *Sunday Post*, *Scottish Sunday Express* (which, like its daily counterpart, is printed in Manchester) and *Scotland on Sunday*. Scottish editions of *The Times*, *The Sun*, *Sunday Times* and *News of the World* are printed in Glasgow.

Periodicals include three monthly illustrated journals, a weekly paper devoted to farming interests, a number of literary journals, and numerous popular magazines.

The British Broadcasting Corporation (BBC), the Independent Television Commission (ITC) and the Radio Authority—the three public bodies licensed to provide television and radio broadcasting services in Britain—operate centres in Scotland. This ensures that Scottish interests and activities receive appropriate coverage in these media. The BBC's Scottish organisation comes under the control of the National Broadcasting Council for Scotland, whose chairman is one of the BBC's national governors. The main radio and television studios are in Glasgow and there are smaller centres in Edinburgh and Aberdeen. BBC Radio Scotland provides a full range of programmes for Scottish audiences, and also contributes a proportion of programmes to the national network. The television department also contributes a proportion of programmes to the national network.

The ITC operates a commercial television service regionally through appointed programme companies. It has centres in Glasgow and Edinburgh (Scottish Television, covering central Scotland) and Aberdeen (Grampian Television, covering north and east Scotland). Programmes from Carlisle in Cumbria (Border Television) cover an area on both sides of the Scotland/England border. As with the BBC, programmes may be designed for local showing only or for transmission on the national network. There are 11 local commercial radio stations.

The Government has set up a Gaelic Television Fund to finance up to 200 hours each year of a wide range of programmes in Gaelic. The first of these programmes will be broadcast in 1993.

Sport and Recreation

Scotland's countryside is naturally suited to a wide range of sports and recreations. Responsibility for the general development of sport rests with the Scottish Sports Council, a government-financed body, which aims to:

—encourage wider participation in sport throughout Scotland;

—foster the provision of new sports facilities and the use of existing sports facilities;

—raise and maintain standards of performance in sport and physical recreation; and

—promote general understanding of the importance of sport and physical recreation in society.

The Council consults with the Scottish Sports Association, which comprises representatives of the governing bodies of sport in Scotland. It also co-operates with Scottish Natural Heritage (see p. 62) and other amenity bodies in planning recreational activities in the countryside. Local authorities are responsible for providing facilities such as playing fields, gymnasia, tennis courts, golf courses, swimming pools and sports centres. There are 54 local sports councils which encourage the development of sport locally—for example, by giving grant aid to local bodies, and organising courses and events.

The Scottish Sports Council operates three national sports centres: Glenmore Lodge near Aviemore, for outdoor sports, including mountain activities; Inverclyde at Largs, for general sports; and a sailing and water sports centre on Cumbrae Isle on the

Firth of Clyde. A government grant of £800,000 over two years was allocated to the Council in 1991 to support an extensive renovation and development programme at Glenmore Lodge.

'Team Sport Scotland' was launched by the Council in May 1991 to promote the development of school-aged team sport, concentrating particularly on strengthening the links between schools, clubs and the community. The initiative was made possible through a special Scottish Office grant of £400,000 in the first year, with a commitment to further funding for another two years. The team sports covered by the project are football, shinty (see below), rugby, cricket, netball, basketball, volleyball and hockey.

At international level a number of recent successes have been achieved by Scottish sportsmen and women, including:

—Liz McColgan, winner of a gold medal in the women's 10,000 metres in the 1991 World Athletics Championships in Tokyo and winner of the inaugural women's world half-marathon championship in September 1992;

—Stephen Hendry, world snooker champion in 1990 and 1992;

—David Smith, winner of a gold medal in the 1991 World Curling Championships;

—Sandy Lyle, who won the United States Masters golf tournament in 1988; and

—the Scotland team at the 1992 world outdoor bowls championships, which won the Leonard Trophy (the team title), together with gold medals in the pairs and fours.

Popular Activities

Among the outdoor activities for which the Scottish terrain offers considerable scope are mountaineering and hill walking, bird watching, pony trekking, trout and salmon fishing, deer stalking and winter and water sports in general. Scotland possesses some of the best salmon rivers in the British Isles and there are opportunities for sea fishing round all the coasts. Deer stalking is mainly a sport of the Highlands, where deer are kept in privately owned deer forests and protected during the close season. Facilities such as forest trails, camping sites and picnic places contribute to the enjoyment of forest and woodland areas. Winter sports are becoming increasingly popular in the Cairngorm Mountains, Glencoe and a number of other areas.

The game of golf originated in Scotland, and there are now more than 400 golf courses, including such famous venues as Turnberry, Troon and St Andrews, which have all hosted the British Open golf championship. The Royal and Ancient Golf Club in St Andrews has taken a major role in the modern development of the game and is the international governing body.

One of the most popular spectator and participation sports is association football, which is played on a full-time basis by 38 clubs. These are divided into three divisions and belong to the Scottish Football League. By 1994 all football grounds in the Premier Division will be required to have all-seated accommodation to comply with government safety recommendations. The same requirement was reviewed in 1992 in respect of certain smaller clubs with lower attendances in the First and Second Divisions being all-seated by 1999. Following the review, the Secretary of State for Scotland confirmed that clubs in the First and Second Divisions may retain standing accommodation for spectators. The Government has offered a contribution of £3.5 million towards the cost of converting Hampden Park, the national football stadium, into an all-seated venue.

Rugby union football is played in the National League and Inter-District Championships. The Five Nations Tournament between Scotland, England, Wales, Ireland and France is contested annually. Scotland last won the Tournament in 1990, and reached the semi-finals of the World Cup in 1991. A £2 million grant to the Scottish Rugby Union was announced by the Government in 1991 for improvements to Murrayfield Stadium in Edinburgh, the venue for international matches.

Hockey and its Highland variation, shinty, are other popular team games. Curling, a winter game similar to bowls but played on ice, is increasing in popularity. For centuries it has been played on frozen lakes, and a number of indoor rinks are also used.

Highland Games, which take place at various centres during the summer, attract large numbers of spectators from all over the world. Sports at these traditional gatherings include tossing the caber, putting the shot and throwing the hammer, as well as athletics and competitions in piping and Highland and Scottish country dancing. The Braemar Gathering on Deeside is one of the best known.

Addresses

The Scottish Office

The Scottish Office, St Andrew's House, Edinburgh EH1 3DE.

The Scottish Office Agriculture and Fisheries Department, Pentland House, 47 Robb's Loan, Edinburgh EH14 1TW.

The Scottish Office Education Department, New St Andrew's House, Edinburgh EH1 3SY.

The Scottish Office Environment Department, St Andrew's House, Edinburgh EH1 3DD.

The Scottish Office Home and Health Department, St Andrew's House, Edinburgh EH1 3DE.

The Scottish Office Industry Department, New St Andrew's House, Edinburgh EH1 3TA.

The Scottish Office Information Directorate, New St Andrew's House, Edinburgh EH1 3TD.

London office for above departments: Dover House, Whitehall, London SW1A 2AU.

Other Departments and Organisations

Ancient Monuments Board for Scotland, 20 Brandon Street, Edinburgh EH3 5RA.

Crofters Commission, 4–6 Castle Wynd, Inverness IV2 3EQ.

Forestry Commission, 231 Corstorphine Road, Edinburgh EH12 7AT.

General Register Office (Scotland), New Register House, Edinburgh EH1 3YT.

Highlands and Islands Enterprise, Bridge House, 20 Bridge Street, Inverness IV1 1QR.

National Galleries of Scotland, The Mound, Edinburgh EH2 2EL.

National Library of Scotland, George IV Bridge, Edinburgh EH1 1EW.

National Museums of Scotland, Chambers Street, Edinburgh EH1 1JF.

Offshore Supplies Office, Alhambra House, 45 Waterloo Street, Glasgow G2 6AS.

Department of the Registers for Scotland, Meadowbank House, 153 London Road, Edinburgh EH8 7AU.

Scottish Community Education Council, West Coates House, 90 Haymarket Terrace, Edinburgh EH12 5LQ.

Scottish Consultative Council on the Curriculum, 17 St John Street, Edinburgh EH8 8DG.

Scottish Enterprise, 120 Bothwell Street, Glasgow G2 7JP.

Scottish Homes, Rosebery House, 9 Haymarket Terrace, Edinburgh EH12 5YA.

Scottish Law Commission, 140 Causewayside, Edinburgh EH9 1PR.

Scottish Natural Heritage, 12 Hope Terrace, Edinburgh EH9 2AS.

Scottish Record Office, HM General Register House, Edinburgh EH1 3YY.

Scottish Sports Council, Caledonia House, South Gyle, Edinburgh EH12 9DQ.

Scottish Tourist Board, 23 Ravelston Terrace, Edinburgh EH4 3EU.

Further Reading

£

FENTON, ALEXANDER.
Scottish Country Life.
2nd edition. ISBN 0 85976 291 2.   John Donald 1989 13.95

FINLAYSON, IAIN. *The Scots.*
ISBN 0 19 282118 0.   Oxford University Press 1988 4.95

FRY, MICHAEL. *Patronage and Principle:*
A Political History of Modern Scotland.
ISBN 0 08 041407 9.   Aberdeen University Press 1991 9.95

SMOUT, T. C. *A Century of the Scottish*
People 1830–1950. ISBN 0 00 686141 5.   Fontana 1987 7.99

People and Society in Scotland.
Vol. 1: *A Social History of Modern Scotland*
1760–1830. Editors: T. M. Devine and
R. Mitchison. ISBN 0 85976 210 6.   John Donald 1988 10.00

Vol 2: *1830–1914.*
Editors: W. H. Fraser and R. J. Morris.
ISBN 0 85976 211 4.   John Donald 1989 12.50

Vol 3: *1914 to the Present Day.*
Editors: A. D. R. Dickinson and
J. H. Treble. ISBN 0 85976 212 2.   John Donald 1991 12.50

Access and Opportunity: A Strategy for
Education and Training. Cm 1530.
ISBN 0 10 115302 3.   HMSO 1991 5.50

Census 1991 Preliminary Report for
Scotland. ISBN 0 11 494180 7.   HMSO 1991 3.80

£

Parents' Charter in Scotland.
The Scottish Office Education Department 1991 Free

Privatisation of the Scottish Electricity
Industry. Cm 327. ISBN 0 10 103272 2. HMSO 1988 2.80

Scotland's Health—A Challenge to Us All.
Scottish Office Home and Health
Department. ISBN 0 11 494218 8. HMSO 1992 19.50

Scotland's Natural Heritage:
The Way Ahead. The Scottish Office 1990 Free

Scottish Enterprise: A New Approach
to Training and Enterprise Creation.
Cm 534. ISBN 0 10 105342 8. HMSO 1988 5.00

The Scottish New Towns: The Way Ahead.
Cm 711. ISBN 0 10 107112 4. HMSO 1989 5.00

The Structure of Local Government in
Scotland. The Scottish Office 1991 Free

The Structure of Local Government in
Scotland: Shaping the New Councils. The Scottish Office 1992 Free

Urban Scotland into the 1990s—2
Years On. The Scottish Office 1990 Free

Discussion and research papers on various topics are published from time to time by the Economics and Statistics Unit of the Scottish Office Industry Department.

Periodical Publications
(annual unless otherwise stated)

Agriculture in Scotland. HMSO

Economic Report on Scottish Agriculture. HMSO

Serving Scotland's Needs.
The Government's Expenditure Plans:
Scotland and Forestry Commission.   HMSO

Health in Scotland.   HMSO

Highlands and Islands Enterprise.   HIE

Locate in Scotland Review.   Scottish Enterprise

Prisons in Scotland.   HMSO

Annual Report of the Registrar-General.   HMSO

Scottish Abstract of Statistics.   HMSO

Scottish Economic Bulletin. (Twice a year)   HMSO

Scottish Enterprise.   SE

Scottish Government Year Book.   Paul Harris

Scottish Tourist Board.   STB

Scottish Office Briefs on various topics, regularly revised, are obtainable from The Scottish Office Information Directorate.

Index

Printed in the UK for HMSO.
Dd.0295923, 2/93, C30, 51-2423, 5673.

CURRENT AFFAIRS:
A MONTHLY SURVEY

Using the latest authoritative information from official and other sources, *Current Affairs* is an invaluable digest of important developments in all areas of British affairs. Focusing on policy initiatives and other topical issues, its factual approach makes it the ideal companion for *Britain Handbook* and *Aspects of Britain*. Separate sections deal with governmental; international; economic; and social, cultural and environmental affairs. A further section provides details of recent documentary sources for these areas. There is also a twice-yearly index.

Annual subscription including index and postage £35·80 net. Binder £4·95.

Buyers of Britain 1993: An Official Handbook *qualify for a discount of 25 per cent on a year's subscription to* Current Affairs *(see next page).*

HMSO Publications Centre
(Mail and telephone orders only)
PO Box 276
LONDON SW8 5DT
Telephone orders: 071 873 9090

THE ANNUAL PICTURE

BRITAIN
1993

AN OFFICIAL HANDBOOK

BRITAIN HANDBOOK

The annual picture of Britain is provided by *Britain: An Official Handbook* - the forty-fourth edition will be published early in 1993. It is the unrivalled reference book about Britain, packed with information and statistics on every facet of British life.

With a circulation of over 20,000 worldwide, it is essential for libraries, educational institutions, business organisations and individuals needing easy access to reliable and up-to-date information, and is supported in this role by its sister publication, *Current Affairs: A Monthly Survey*.

Approx. 500 pages; 24 pages of colour illustrations; 16 maps; diagrams and tables throughout the text; and a statistical section. Price £19·50.

Buyers of Britain 1993: An Official Handbook *have the opportunity of a year's subscription to* Current Affairs *at 25 per cent off the published price of £35·80. They will also have the option of renewing their subscription next year at the same discount. Details in each copy of* Handbook, *from HMSO Publications Centre and at HMSO bookshops (see back of title page).*